SELF-PUBLISH YOUR BOOK using LIBREOFFICE

SELF-PUBLISH YOUR BOOK

using

LIBREOFFICE

HARWOOD W. LOOMIS

SELF-PUBLISH YOUR BOOK
Using
LIBREOFFICE

ISBN: 978-1-957418-22-3

Published by:
THE ELDERSLIE PRESS
172 Peck Hill Road
Woodbridge, Connecticut 06525
United States of America

Acknowledgments

As a direct result of the complexity of setting up page styles in LibreOffice Writer, this book by necessity became longer than I originally anticipated. Added length brings with it added opportunities to make mistakes. I am indebted to two other authors who use Writer to self-publish books, Steven Arseneault and Kevin Batchelor, for taking time from their own writing to review my manuscript and offer suggestions on things I had missed or that needed to be explained more completely.

Contents

SELF-PUBLISH YOUR BOOK

using

LIBREOFFICE

Introduction

A decision faced by all fledgling authors is how to get their book published. There are thousands of people who want to be authors, and together I'm sure they write millions, if not billions, of words every year. ALL of these hopeful authors are competing against each other as well as against books published by established authors and mainstream, commercial publishing juggernauts. There aren't any major, traditional publishers who accept unsolicited manuscripts from rookie writers. The only way to get a manuscript accepted by a major publisher is through an agent—but most agents are overwhelmed with manuscripts and queries, too, so the odds are heavily against even getting an agent to read your manuscript if you are a new author who doesn't have a solid track record.

The invention of print-on-demand delivery for printed books has revolutionized the publishing industry and made it possible for thousands of amateur and undiscovered writers to not only see their books in print, but to see them offered for sale on the Internet through vendors such as Amazon, Barnes and Noble, and a host of others. Amazon KDP is the biggest player in this field, by a significant margin, but there are reasons why authors might choose either to use another service to publish their book, or to release their book through multiple vendors simultaneously. This book isn't about how to decide which print-on-demand service to use. That's a marketing decision, and each author's situation and expectations are different, making it a very personal decision, as well.

Once an author makes the decision to self-publish, the next decision to be made is how to create the manuscript and, after that, how to take the finished manuscript from a raw computer file to a final format that's ready to be uploaded to Amazon KDP or to another print-on-demand service for printing. This can be done in Microsoft Word and, in fact, I have written a book that explains exactly how to do it using Word. But Microsoft Office is an expensive program (or suite of programs), and not everyone can afford it. Beyond that, while a word processor such as Word is good for writing the raw manuscript, there are a great many experts (both real experts and self-professed experts) who proclaim that in order to properly format a book for print you have to use expensive software such as Adobe *InDesign, Scrivener, Affinity Publisher,* or *Atticus.* Other experts advise authors who want to self-publish to use a free program from Amazon called *Kindle Create.* There are other programs, too, that can be used to transform a raw manuscript into a finished book layout; some are free, while others are commercial software that are available only by purchase or subscription.

I'm the first to admit that a program such as *InDesign* is invaluable if the end product is going to be an expensive, high-end book for which the minute, intricate details of the book's interior formatting are as important as the book's content. For most self-published authors, that's simply not the case. *InDesign* is expensive—very expensive. And it's not for sale; *InDesign* is only available by subscription, which means to use it you have to rent it, at a cost of $239.88 per year (or more, depending on the plan). That's a lot of money for most beginning authors, and the monetary cost doesn't factor in the extra time needed to learn how to use the software.

Most authors just want to tell the story, and to get it out there so that people can read it. Ideally, we want it to look professional enough that a reader's first impression when they open the book won't be, "Oh, my God! This book must have been created by a kindergartner!" Fortunately, we don't need *InDesign*; we can accomplish perfectly acceptable formatting using the same word processing software we use to write the manuscript. It's not even difficult; it just requires taking the time needed to learn how to lay out a book for print, and caring enough about the work to make it look as professional as possible. Not only that, the good news for people who can't afford or who don't want to spend the money to buy (or subscribe to) Microsoft Office is that there are entirely *free* programs available that can not only facilitate drafting the manuscript, they can also be used to format the book to be print-ready. The result, all from one *free* program, will be good enough that only a professional book designer will know your book wasn't designed by a professional.

There are three *free* programs that rival Microsoft Word in features and flexibility: LibreOffice Writer, OpenOffice Writer, and FreeOffice TextMaker. All three are components of office suites that include a word processor, a spreadsheet, and a presentations program. LibreOffice and OpenOffice also include a drawing program and a database but, since the major tool for producing a book is the word processor, that's what this book will focus on.

LibreOffice is not only free, it is also "open source." This means that not only is the software free, the source code is also free, and can be downloaded and modified by anyone who has sufficient programming capabilities. This doesn't matter to most authors, but those who are particularly concerned with computer security often favor using open source software whenever possible. Further, LibreOffice is available for Windows, for macOS, and for Linux. In fact, LibreOffice is bundled as the standard office suite application in many distros of Linux.

LibreOffice and OpenOffice both had their beginning in an earlier office suite named StarOffice. After multiple changes of ownership, StarOffice became OpenOffice. When development of OpenOffice lagged, another group created LibreOffice as a "fork" of OpenOffice in 2010. Even today, LibreOffice and OpenOffice look, feel, and function very much the same. This book will explain how anyone can use LibreOffice Writer to write, format, and self-publish their book, from manuscript to final upload, without having to spend *any* money to buy software. Most of this information should also apply to OpenOffice.

A word of caution: LibreOffice (and OpenOffice) Writer rival Microsoft Word in capability but, once beyond just opening the program and typing into the default blank page that appears on the screen, the process of formatting a document such as a book is very different from Word. Each different page type (title page, front matter pages, chapter first pages, chapter left pages, and chapter right pages) has to be configured individually.

For this reason, I strongly advise authors using Writer to create a template (or multiple templates, for those who publish books in different trim sizes). Once created, the master copy of the template should be saved. For new books, the template can be used in two ways:

One way is to write and edit the manuscript in standard manuscript format (or unformatted) and then, when the book is ready to be formatted for print, copy and paste each chapter and section from the manuscript into the template as unformatted text. This allows the formatting of the template to control the appearance of the text.

The other way to use a template is to simply write the book directly into the template. This means that, while writing, the author immediately sees how the words will appear on the printed page. The author will instantly and continuously have chapter lengths and word counts, can see how the words will flow to the reader, and will have a real-time visual indicator of progress.

Either way, the use of a template with LibreOffice Writer saves the time that would otherwise have to be expended formatting each and every different page type, for each and every book.

An important caveat: when using a template in Writer, in order to have headers work properly it is very important to use manual breaks (not just typing CTRL+Enter) for chapter breaks. This is explained starting on page 58.

I — Getting The Software

The LibreOffice suite is a very complete suite of office applications, including not only the usual word processor, spreadsheet, and presentations programs but also a relational database module and a module that's named "Draw" but which actually functions as much like a desktop publishing program as it does a drawing program..

LibreOffice, being completely free, allows installation on as many devices as the user may have. There is no license or activation key required. Simply download the software and install it. Currently, for Windows LibreOffice is only available in a 64-bit version. As this is being written, the current stable version is 26.2.2. As of release 25.8, in August of 2025, 32-bit Windows versions were dropped. The current version of OpenOffice is 4.1.16. In contrast with LibreOffice, for Windows OpenOffice is only available in a 32-bit version. Both 32-bit and 64-bit versions are available for Linux.

LibreOffice includes automatic hyphenation, spell-check with auto-correct, a grammar checker, and a thesaurus. It reads and writes both .doc and .docx file formats (used by Microsoft Word), as well as the .odt file format (used by LibreOffice).

The OpenOffice version of Writer can open files in the Microsoft Word .doc and .docx formats, but can only save to the older .doc file format. This can be a problem if the publishing service you use doesn't accept the .doc file format. Amazon KDP can accept both .doc and .docx. Barnes and Noble Press also accepts both for e-books, but requires a PDF for print. Draft2Digital accepts both. Kobo accepts both .doc and .docx formats, as well as .odt. Some other self-publishing platforms will only accept the newer .docx file format, not the old .doc format.

I have my copy of Writer set to use the .docx format as the default file format, because I frequently exchange documents with people who use Microsoft Office. If I were to use it strictly for writing and publishing, I would leave the default file format set for the native .odt file format.

Pretty much all the print-on-demand services accept (and recommend) uploading the book interior as a PDF rather than as a word processing file. This locks in the formatting so the finished book will look exactly the way you laid it out. LibreOffice has the built-in capability of exporting to PDF (including to PDF/A), and also allows exporting directly to the .epub digital book format.

That's a lot of functionality in an entirely free software package.

Obtaining the software is as simple as downloading the installation file and running it. The first time you start the software there will be a pop-up box offering user tips. There is an option to turn this off so that it will not appear in the future when the program starts. I prefer to leave it active.

There is also a help file that can be downloaded and installed as an add-on to the program.

Once the software has been installed, there should be a new icon on the desktop to launch LibreOffice.

The link to the LibreOffice web site for downloading the installation file is:

https://www.libreoffice.org/download/

2 — The Manuscript

Once the software has been installed, it's time to write the book. Writer offers some tools to make that job easier. LibreOffice Writer offers a very flexible and useful sidebar. When the sidebar is activated, it can displays the character styles, paragraph styles and page styles, which facilitates formatting. (The sidebar can also display a variety of other information, the most useful of which is probably the document navigator.)

As in Microsoft Word, Writer has a built-in spelling checker that underlines in red any words that aren't found in its dictionary. Writer also includes a grammar checker. My experience using the grammar checker built into Microsoft Word was that the grammar checker was totally useless, and I disabled it because it interfered with my style of writing. For this reason, I immediately disabled the grammar checker in Writer and I don't use it at all. Writers who feel they might want the assistance of a computer grammar checker can activate the grammar checker by clicking on a check box at the bottom of the pop-up dialogue for spell check. If the built-in grammar checker isn't sufficient, there is a free app called *Language Tool*. A free version of *Language Tool* is available that runs on-line, in your web browser, and there is also a free desktop app that can be downloaded for use under Windows or macOS.

I happen to be a visually-oriented person so, unlike most writers, I prefer to set up the format for a book before I start. This allows me to actually see how the book is going to appear to readers as I progress. This approach is more suitable for non-fiction, especially for books that will include illustration, photos, and/or charts and graphs. For writing a novel, most writers will probably find it less constricting to start working on a standard 8½ by 11 page size using Times New Roman as the font in 11-point or 12-point size, and simply write. All that can be changed during the formatting stage, so there is no need to be concerned about it while writing the story.

If you plan to submit the manuscript to agents or commercial publishers, then it absolutely should be set up in a standard manuscript format. If the publisher or agent has their own format requirements, be sure to follow them. If there are no specific requirements, the following criteria are a good starting point:

- Set the margins to 1-inch all around — top. Bottom, and both sides
- Use Times New Roman 12-point type
- Indent the first line of each paragraph ½ inch
- Set the line spacing to double space
- Use left justification only. Do NOT use full justification
- Put a header at the top right, including your last name, a dash, the title, a dash, and the page number
- Use ONE space after a period, not two. (Using two spaces after periods is a carry-over from the days of mechanical typewriters.)
- Begin each chapter on a new page, with the chapter number and/or title about one-third of the way down the page
- Show breaks in the action or timeline within a chapter with a blank line, with the # symbol centered on the line
- To finish the manuscript, put "The End" on a separate line following the last line of the text.

The first page of the manuscript will be the title page. This page does not get a header or a page number. The title page should include:

- The author's name and contact information in the upper left-hand corner. Include telephone number and e-mail address.
- The book title and sub-title, between one-third and one-half down the page, center-justified
- The author's name again (or pen name, if used, also center justified)
- The word count

That's the basic layout for a manuscript. Most agents and publishers will either accept this format, or have their own requirements which should be very similar to these.

In Microsoft Word, the default paragraph style is called "Normal" and the default tab stop spacing is one-half inch. LibreOffice Writer calls the default paragraph style "Default Paragraph Style" and, as with Microsoft Word, the default tab stop spacing is 0.5 inches. Do NOT use the tab key to indent the first lines of paragraphs in manuscripts. Instead, modify the default paragraph style to automatically indent the first line of new paragraphs. To accomplish this, be sure the sidebar is visible, with the paragraph styles displayed. Right click on the Default Paragraph Style, then click "Edit Style" in the pop-up box:

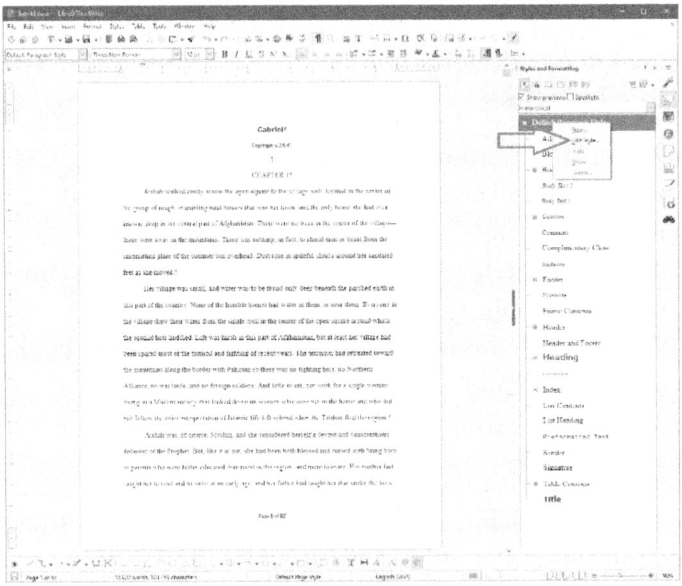

This opens the pop-up dialogue box in which you can set the parameters for the default paragraph style. The options for setting tab stops is near the bottom in the menu on the left-hand side:

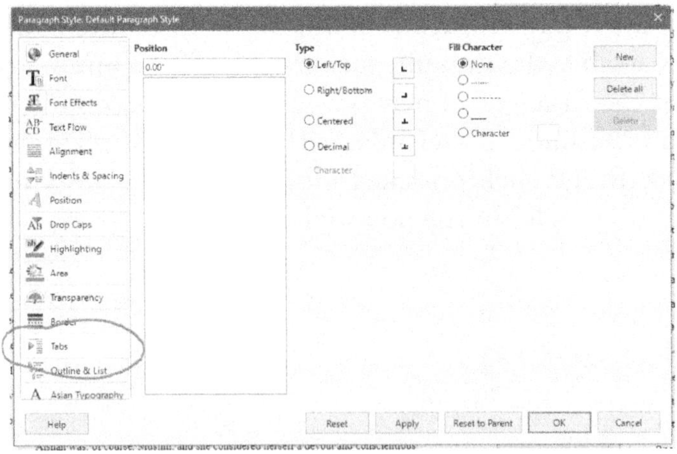

When it's time to format the book interior for print, additional paragraph styles will become more important. For just writing the manuscript, this is all that's needed.

Each new chapter should begin on a new page. There are multiple ways to accomplish this; one is just plain wrong, one is okay, and the third method that I recommend for Word is not available in LibreOffice Writer: That means in LibreOffice Writer method 2 is the only option.

1. DON'T just keep hitting the enter key (line breaks) to keep entering blank lines until the text jumps to the new page. That way is wrong by anyone's criteria, but there are people who still think of a computer word processor like a fancy electric typewriter who do this. Just ... DON'T.
2. The second way to jump to a new page is to hold down the CTRL key and press the ENTER key. This inserts a page break code into the file. This feature works exactly the same in Writer as it does in Microsoft Word, so people familiar with Word will have no trouble doing this one. HOWEVER—a page break is not a chapter break. As an alternate, from the menu bar across the top of the screen click on Insert > Manual Break. (See discussion beginning on page 59.)
3. In Word, the third way to jump to a new page is to insert a section break. Readers who are accustomed to using Word and who know about section breaks, BEWARE! What Word calls a section break does not exist in LibreOffice Writer. In Writer, "section" means something very different from what it means in Word. Use method number 2 for chapter breaks in Writer.

~ ~ ~ ~ ~

Now it's time to start writing. Once the manuscript has been completed and edited, it will be time to take the finished manuscript and format it for print if you aren't going to submit it to agents for publication through the traditional publishing route.

3 — Trim Size

The first step in formatting any book for print is deciding what size the book will be, what the physical dimensions will be. In book publishing, this is referred to as "trim size." The name derives from the way printed books are produced and assembled. The individual pages are printed on larger sheets of paper that each typically hold four printed pages. These larger sheets are called *folios*. The pages are slightly larger than the intended final size of the book. They are folded and then bound together to create the book. After assembly, the edges are trimmed to the final size.

Choosing a trim size is both an art and a science. All of the popular print-on-demand services offer a range of standard trim sizes from which to choose. Amazon KDP also allows custom trim sizes but, since most other print-on-demand services do not, unless you plan to offer your book exclusively through Amazon it is best to use one of the standard trim sizes that all the services offer.

The basic rule of thumb for determining what trim size to use is to look at other books of the same type or genre as your book fits into, and to choose a trim size that the majority of your competition uses. There's a reason for this. This is not a situation where it's good to stand out from the crowd. There are a lot of books available today. People who read books of a particular genre become accustomed to a general size and style, so a new book that's drastically different from what they have read and enjoyed in the past is less likely to appeal to these potential buyers. If you don't know what size other books of the same genre are, spend a few minutes at a bookstore or in the books aisle at the local supermarket with a ruler or a tape measure to find out what size publishers are using for books in the same genre as your book. (This is also a good opportunity to get a feel for what types of cover design are popular for that genre, but that is beyond the scope of this book.)

The following are some general criteria for trim size:

5" x 8"	Novellas (short novels); general fiction
5.25" x 8"	General fiction
5.5" x 8.5"	Fiction and non-fiction
6" x 9"	Fiction and Non-fiction; longer books

(Larger pages help reduce page count. Some sources say 6" x 9" is the most commonly used trim size for books in the United States.)

~ ~ ~ ~ ~

Not even all those sizes are offered by all three of the most popular print-on-demand services: Amazon KDP, Barnes and Noble Press, and Draft2Digital. Amazon KDP and Barnes and Noble Press both offer all four trim sizes in paperback, but they only offer 5.5" x 8.5" and 6" x 9" in hardcover. Draft2Digital does not offer the 5.25" x 8" trim size. For maximum flexibility in printing and distribution, this means it is best to choose a trim size of 5" x 8", 5.5" x 8.5", or 6" x 9".

If your proposed book is something that you think will fall into the "mass market" category (those smaller books that are often found in revolving racks at convenience stores and similar outlets), Barnes and Noble Press offers the following standard trim sizes:

4" x 6"
4.25" x 7"
4.37" x 7"

Neither Amazon KDP nor Draft2Digital offers any of those sizes as standard trim sizes. Amazon KDP allows custom trim sizes, which will allow matching one of those sizes if you wish to publish through both Amazon KDP and Barnes and Noble Press. Draft2Digital does not appear to offer custom trim sizes.

To further confuse the issue, although Barnes and Noble Press says the 4.25" x 7" size is the "mass market" trim size ... it isn't. I have measured many mass market paperback books, and the most customary trim size by an overwhelming margin is actually 4.13" x 6.75".

There is also a new trim size that several mass market publishers have recently introduced to the marketplace: what Kensington Publishing Corporation has named the "Mass Max" format. This is slightly larger than the traditional mass market trim size, and the goal is to give prospective buyers a feeling that they are getting a bit more than what the traditional mass market size books offer. This new trim size is 4.75" x 7". At this time, none of the major print-on-demand services offer this as a standard trim size, and none of them appears to have any plans to introduce it. This means if you want to publish your book in that trim size, at the moment the only option is to use a custom trim size from Amazon KDP.

Once you have chosen the trim size and decided what dimensions you want to use for the margins, you are ready to proceed with setting up the page layouts.

4 — Page Layout

Before beginning to set up the format of the book interior, it's important to understand that LibreOffice Writer requires a very different approach than Microsoft Word. For anyone who is accustomed to using Word, it can be difficult to wrap your head around just how different LibreOffice Writer really is in this regard. The differences aren't apparent when you're just typing away at a bunch of words on a plain 8½" x 11" page, but the differences become very real, very quickly, when it comes to formatting a book for print.

Perhaps the best way to describe the difference is that in Word, for overall page layout, we essentially format the *document.* In setting paper size, orientation, and margin dimensions in Word we can choose whether the settings apply to the entire document or just to a specific section but, in general, most people just set these parameters (if they bother to depart from the standard template at all) at the start of creating a document and then just start typing. The settings then carry forward through the entire document, on every new page that's created. Within a section, setting the page size and margins once instantly applies those settings to every page in the section, or to every page in the document.

LibreOffice works in an entirely different way. In LibreOffice Writer, each page that may need any aspect of its formatting to be unique *must* have a page style defined for that particular type of page. If anything is different—Roman numeral page numbers in the front matter, different margins on left-hand and right-hand pages, no headers on first pages of chapters, different headers on left-hand and right-hand pages—it requires a dedicated page style to be created.

Setting up the page styles isn't rocket science, but for anyone accustomed to the way Microsoft Word handle page formatting, it's a quantum shift in approach. For anyone who expects or who hopes to write more than one book, I strongly advise setting up the first book as a template, and keeping a copy of that template for use with all future books. Being a visually-oriented person, I prefer to write in a formatted template so that, as I write, I always see what my book is going to look like. Not everyone is happy or even able to work like that, but I know at least one successful science fiction writer who does exactly that; he writes directly into his pre-formatted template.

~ ~ ~ ~ ~

In Microsoft Word, the page size is set from the "Layout" tab on the ribbon menu, from which all the variables for the finished book can be set in one place, applicable to the entire file. Unfortunately, LibreOffice Writer doesn't work that way. Writer depends on creating separate page styles for pages with headers, for pages without headers, for chapter first pages, for left-hand body pages, and for right-hand body pages. There is no global way to set all of the page styles together or, in fact, to set any parameters for pages globally. Each page style has to be defined individually. In order to prepare for setting up the necessary page styles, you first have to understand the various parts that make up the entirety of a printed book. Some parts should have headers, some parts should not. Some parts should have footers, other parts should not. Page numbers for most (but not all!) pages in the front matter should use lower case Roman numerals rather than Arabic numerals.

In LibreOffice Writer, all this has to be set up one page style at a time. In Writer, the setup for each page style includes specifying the style to be applied to the following page, which means that any page styles that are not predefined in Writer have to be defined. Writer includes several page styles that are applicable to printed books, but their settings need to be modified to suit a book. This may require setting up most parameters for a style, creating a new style, and then going back into an earlier style to set the following page style. Let's look at the basic parts of a book and their essential parameters:

Front matter

- Half title page—Always a right-hand page, with no header, no footer, no page number
- Title page— Always a right-hand page, with no header, no footer, no page number
- Copyright page— Always a left-hand page, with no header, no footer, no page number
- Dedication—Optional. Always starts on a right-hand page. No headers. Page number in bottom margin, lower case Roman numerals.
- Epigraph— Optional. Always a right-hand page. No headers. Page number in bottom margin, lower case Roman numerals.
- Contents—Always starts on a right-hand page. No headers. Page number in bottom margin, lower case Roman numerals.
- Foreword— Optional. Always starts on a right-hand page. No headers. Page number in bottom margin, lower case Roman numerals.
- Preface— Optional. Always starts on a right-hand page. No headers. Page number in bottom margin, lower case Roman numerals.

- Acknowledgements— Optional. Always starts on a right-hand page. No headers. Page number in bottom margin, lower case Roman numerals.
- Half title page— Always a right-hand page, with no header, no footer, no page number

Book body

- Chapter first pages—Ideally, always start on a right-hand page. Less common: allow chapters to start on left-hand or right-hand page. No header. Page number in bottom margin, in Arabic numerals.
- Chapter body pages—Mirrored margins. Alternating headers on left-hand and right-hand pages. Page numbers in Arabic numerals, either in headers or in footer.

Back matter

- About the author— Optional. Always starts on a right-hand page. No headers. Page number in bottom margin, lower case Roman numerals.
- Other books by the author— Optional. Always starts on a right-hand page. No headers. Page number in bottom margin, lower case Roman numerals.

Once the trim size has been selected, the next step is to establish the margins and layout of the interior pages. Although each of the major print-on-demand services has slightly different suggested criteria for these dimensions, it is possible to select a single set of dimensions that will work for all of them. But, first, we need to understand the terminology that applies.

Every page has a top margin, a bottom margin, and two side margins. For a single page, the side margins are simple "left" and "right." But a book is formatted with the pages viewed as pairs, so the names of the margins change. With the book held open, the side margins at the extreme left and the extreme right are referred to as the "outside" margins, while the two margins nearest to the spine of the book are referred to as the "inside" margins. The top and bottom margins, of course, remain the same.

The layout of a basic page includes the block of text that makes up the story (the book body), together with top, bottom inside and outside margins:

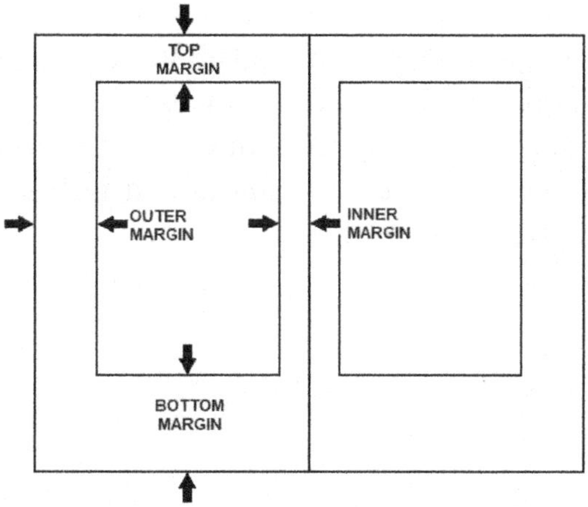

In a classically-designed book, the page layout considers both facing pages together and sets the inside and outside margins such that the two inside margins together equal the width of the outside margin:

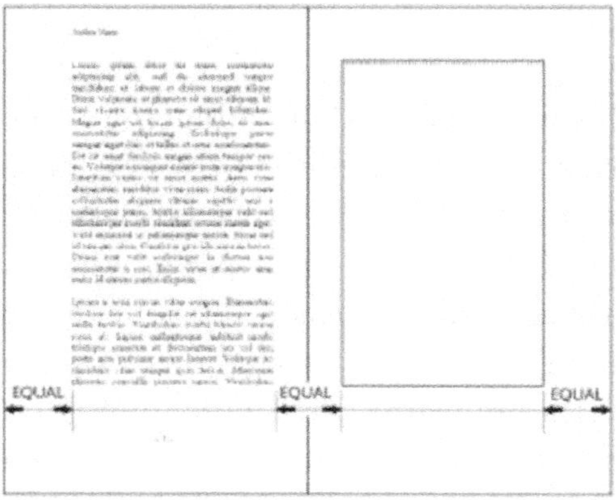

As a general rule, this means that the inside margins would be approximately half the width of the outside margins. But most books—especially paperback books—don't open completely and lie flat when opened. A portion of each page is glued or sewn together in the binding process, so when the book is opened the inside edges of the pages stay together and the reader can't view all the way to the absolute edge of the page. Book makers and book designers allow for the portion of each page that is "lost" to the binding process. This extra space is referred to as the "gutter."

The next diagram shows the same page size as in the previous two diagrams, but with the added gutter allowance shown to illustrate the concept.

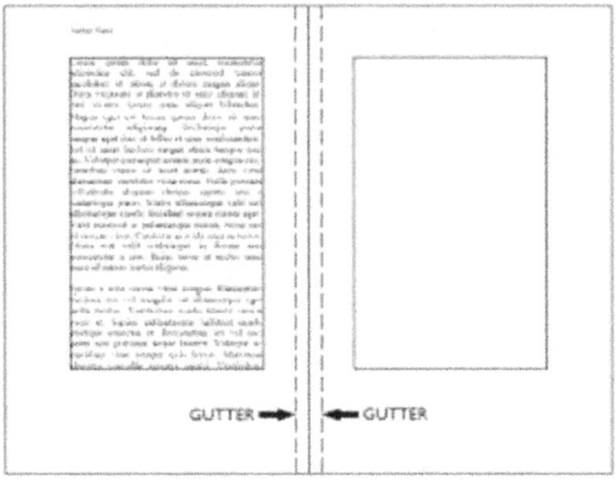

For a self-published author, adhering to classical book design theories should not be the primary concern. Margins created according to classical layout guides are overly large; this results in less text on each page, which means more pages and higher printing costs. For the typical book, the goal is to keep the margins as small as practical, while ensuring that the margins are wide enough to pass the printer's quality checks and also so the text doesn't appear to be uncomfortably crowded onto the pages.

My experience has been that Amazon's guidelines for margins are slightly smaller than desirable (and, for longer books, I have found that margins set to Amazon's minimum dimension won't pass Amazons' own automated quality check). At the end of this chapter, I provide a table with what I have found to be workable margins for the three most common trim sizes. Using these dimensions should allow your book to look like a professional book, and to pass the quality checks on Amazon KDP, Barnes and Noble Press, and Draft2Digital. How to set the gutter dimension varies depending on what program you use.

You can also get an idea of what margins to use by looking at books for sale in the genre your book will fall into. Check a half dozen or so books and make note of what their margins are. If your margins are set to the same dimensions, your printed book will feel comfortable to readers of that genre.

The dimensions set forth in the following table should work for all print-on-demand services. These dimensions are based on having headers that may include the book title, author, and/or chapter title in the header, with page numbers in the footer. For novels, some publishers save space by incorporating page numbers into the headers. In this case, the bottom margin can be reduced to perhaps 0.50" or even slightly less.

Suggested Page Layout Dimensions:

5" x 8"	Inner Margin	0.50"
	Outer Margin	0.50"
	Gutter	0.20"
	Top Margin	0.75"
	Bottom Margin	0.75"
	Header Margin	0.30
	Footer Margin	0.30

5.5" x 8.5"	Inner Margin	0.55"
	Outer Margin	0.55"
	Gutter	0.20
	Top Margin	0.75"
	Bottom Margin	0.75"
	Header Margin	0.30"
	Footer Margin	0.30"
6" x 9"	Inner Margin	0.60"
	Outer Margin	0.60"
	Gutter	0.20"
	Top Margin	0.75"
	Bottom Margin	0.75"
	Header Margin	0.30"
	Footer Margin	0.30"

Word processing programs default to a single page layout; the format has to be changed for a book layout with facing (or "mirrored") pages. In LibreOffice Writer, the layout for each individual page style has to be set independently. A page style has to be defined for pages that don't have headers, for left-hand pages that have headers, for right-hand pages that have headers, for pages with Roman numerals for page numbers, and for pages that he Arabic numerals for page numbers.

Once understood, this approach allows a lot of flexibility in formatting a book. However, it's completely different from the way most word processors function, it's time-consuming, and it's extremely counter-intuitive.

Setting up the format for each page style starts with clicking on "Format" in the Writer menu bar, then clicking on "Page Style." Some page styles are already included as defaults. These are:

- Default Page Style
- Endnote
- Envelope
- First Page
- Footnote
- HTML
- Index
- Landscape
- Left Page
- Right page

For fiction, Endnote, Envelope, Footnote, HTML, Index, and Landscape won't apply and can be ignored. (They can't be deleted because they are defaults. In non-fiction books, especially historical or legal texts, there probably will be either footnotes or endnotes.) I like to use the Default Page Style as the page style for pages that won't have either a header or a footer. This means, usually, the half title pages (if used), the title page, and the copyright page.

Because the pages used the most in any book are the left-hand and right-hand pages of the book body and the chapter first pages, it makes sense to modify the pre-defined First Page, Left Page, and Right Page styles to the setting for your book. Again (I can't stress this enough), in Writer *every* dimension and attribute must be set individually for each and every page style.

To modify an existing page style from the menu bar at the top of the screen, choose "Format" > "Page Style." This opens a dialogue window with several tabs along the left side from which every attribute of the page style can be set. If the style selection sidebar is active, the same settings dialogue window can be accessed by right clicking on the name of the style you wish to edit.

The Page Style dialogue window includes tabs to set or to adjust the attributes, or parameters, for each different page style. To properly set up a book in LibreOffice Writer, *all* the parameters for page style *must* be specified for each different type of page that will appear in the book. Especially in setting up custom page styles for pages that are part of the front matter, it may be necessary to create a style, then create another style, and then go back to a previously created style to set the style for the following page. (These options are slightly different in the OpenOffice version of Writer, but the principle that they must all be defined individually for each page style is the same.)

It's a LOT of work. The best advice is to do it once, then save a copy as a template so it will always be available for future books.

~ ~ ~ ~ ~

Setting page parameters

General

When creating a new page style, this is the tab where you give the style a name, and where you specify what page style follows this page. When editing a pre-defined page style, the name of the style cannot be changed but the style for the next page can be changed.

Page

This is the tab where the page dimensions (paper size and orientation) and margins are set. In addition, this is where the page location is set: for pages that should only be right-hand pages, this is where that is specified. Lastly, this is where the format for page numbers is specified.

In the U.S., the default is a page size of 8.5" x 11"; for the rest of the world, the default is A4.

Area

This tab is used to specify a background color or pattern for pages. For most books, this tab is not used.

Transparency

This tab is where the transparency of page backgrounds is set. For most books, this tab is not used.

Header

This tab is used to specify whether pages of this page style will display a header, and to set the distance between the header and the body text. It is NOT where the content of headers is specified—only whether or not the page style allows a header. As a general rule of thumb, left-hand and right-hand pages of the book body should have headers activated. Chapter first pages, front matter pages, and back matter pages generally should not have headers activated—unless the page numbers are going to be placed in the headers.

Footer

Except for half title pages, the title page, and the copyright page, every page should have a page number. Page numbers for front matter pages should be lower case Roman numerals. All other page numbers should be Arabic numerals. When page numbers are in the headers, the first page of each new chapter does not get a header. Some authors simply omit the page number on chapter first pages, but the more correct approach is to put the page number in the footer on chapter first pages, even if all other pages have the page number in the headers.

Border

The appearance of a book can be enhanced by placing borders on some or all pages. If a border is desired, this tab allows specifying all the parameters of a page border.

- Line Arrangement: The five icons in the Presets field allow choosing to display no border, a border on all four sides, a border only on the vertical sides, a border on the top and bottom only, or a border on the left side only. For more flexibility, the User-Defined field functions like specifying cell borders in a spreadsheet program like Microsoft Excel. Using this field, it is possible to select which sides of the page should display a border by clicking on each side individually.
- Line: The "Style" field offers a drop-down menu offering a variety of solid, dashed, and double lines that can be selected as page border lines. The line types, colors, and thicknesses can be set individually for the border on each side of the page.
- Padding: This setting adjusts the amount of white space between page borders and the text. It is important to be aware that when borders are selected, the borders will be drawn at the page margins set under the "Page" tab (above). The amount of space available for text is thus reduced. The larger the Padding dimensions are set, the less space will be left for text.
- Shadow Style: Lastly, when borders are selected, it is then possible to specify a shadow for the border, and to adjust the width of the shadow.

Columns

This tab is used to specify multiple columns, to set the widths of multiple columns, to set the spacing between columns, and to specify whether or not there is to be a vertical line separating columns. This setting *cannot* be used to format a short section of multi-column text on a page that is otherwise formatted as single-column body text. Thus, for most books, leave the number of columns at the default setting of '1' and do not change or enter any other information for the other fields on this tab.

Footnote

This tab allows changing the specifications for the horizontal line separating footnotes from the body test on the page. It also provides an option to limit the amount of vertical space on the page may be used by footnotes.

Text Grid

In professional book design, pages are set up with what is called a "baseline grid," and text on all pages is set with the baseline of the text aligned to the baseline grid. This ensures that text on facing pages always aligns horizontally across pages. This setting in LibreOffice Writer does the same thing. The default setting is no grid. When grid lines are activated, text will align to the grid lines and thus will align across the binding between left-hand and right-hand pages. LibreOffice offers this feature primarily for working with foreign languages such as Japanese. For books in English and western languages, the Text Grid feature is not needed and I recommend not using it.

~ ~ ~ ~ ~

The following spells out the settings for each page style likely to be found in printed books. It's long and it's boring, but it has to be done so buckle up.

Half Title Pages

Half title pages are completely optional and most self-published books don't use them. On the other hand, a large percentage of traditionally published books do use them. It adds an extra page to help protect the title page, and I like to think that it makes to book look a bit more professional. Just remember that if you use one half title page immediately inside the front cover, you should also include a second half title page at the end of the front matter, before the start of the body of the book.

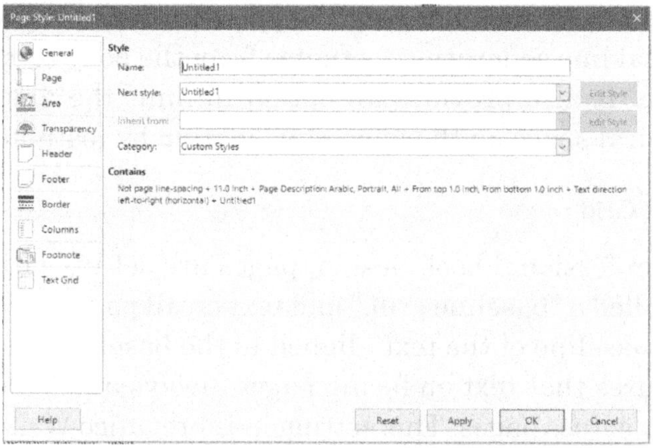

The pre-defined page styles in LibreOffice do not include a style for a half title page, so it has to be created as a new style. This is done from the Styles and Formatting sidebar. If the sidebar is not visible, go to the menu bar, click the "Styles" tab, and then click on "Manage Styles" at the bottom of the drop-down menu. This opens the sidebar. Be sure the "Page Styles" icon is activated. The display will be a list of the styles currently defined in the document. To add a new style, right click anywhere in the sidebar, and select "New." This opens the dialogue box from which all the parameters of the new page style are defined.

General

Because this will be a new page style, both the style name and the style of the following page can be set. For the page style Name, I use "Half Title." It's simple, and it avoids confusion. For Next Style, however, it's not as simple. The page following the first half title page will be the title page, but the page following the second half title page in a book is the first page of the book body. To keep it simple, for this page style I use "Default Page Style" as the Next Style.

There is nothing else to be set on this tab. Leave the Category field set for "Custom Style."

Page

This tab is the most important tab in editing or creating page styles. This is where all the important dimensions and attributes of the style are set. Pay careful attention to these settings, because *most* of these parameters will be the same for all other page styles in the book.

- Paper Format: Enter the dimensions for the trim size selected for the book (5" x 8", 6" x 9", etc.), and be sure the Orientation is set for Portrait. Leave Text Direction set for "Left-to-right" (the default) unless the book is in a language that is written and read right-to-left (such as, for example, Arabic and Hebrew).
- Margins: Enter the margin dimensions decided on for the body text of the book (ignoring headers and footers, since a half title page doesn't have a header or a footer). In LibreOffice, the gutter dimension is also entered here, as a separate dimension. OpenOffice does not have a field to enter a gutter dimension, so the gutter has to be added to the left (or inside) margin. I like to start with a gutter dimension of 0.15" (4 mm); for a very thick book, this may need to be increased.
- Layout Settings: A half title page is always a right-hand page, so for Page Layout choose "Only Right."

A half title page doesn't display a page number, so ignore the field for Page Numbers. Leave the Gutter Position field set to the default of "Left."

Area

This this tab is for setting a background color, texture/pattern, or image that will cover the entire area of all page designated with this page style. For most books it is not used. Leave the "None" options box at the top selected.

Transparency

Unless a background color has been selected, this tab is not used. When a background color, pattern, or image has been selected, this tab allows adjusting the transparency of the background color, pattern, or image. For most books, this setting will not be used.

Header

A half title page does not display a header. Leave the box for "Header On" unchecked.

Footer

A half title page does not display a footer. Leave the box for "Footer On" unchecked.

Border

Most books won't use a border, so nothing on this tab needs to be changed. The appearance of a book can be enhanced by placing borders on some or all pages. If a border is desired, this tab allows specifying all the parameters of a page border, as described beginning on page 31, above.

Columns

The Columns tab in the Page Style settings dialogue box affects the entire area of each page using the page style being created or edited. A half title page only has one column. Do not change anything on this tab.

Footnote

Footnotes will never appear on a half title page. Do not change anything on this tab.

Text Grid

Ignore this tab.

Title Page

The pre-defined page styles in LibreOffice do not include a style for a title page so, like the half title pages, it has to be created as a new style. This is done exactly the same as described for the half title pages, beginning on page 33.

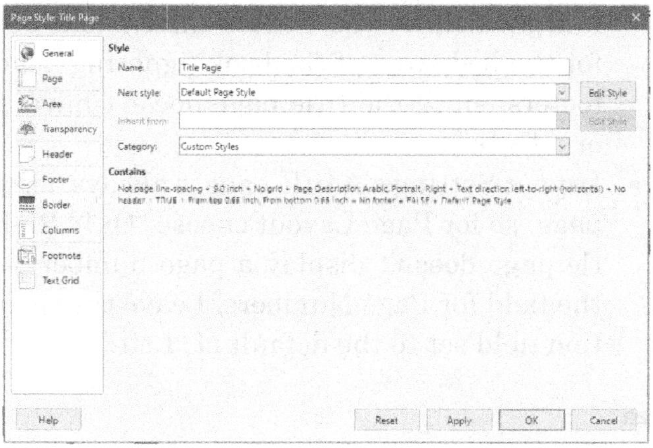

General

Because this will be a new page style, both the style name and the style of the following page can be set. For the page style Name, I use "Title Page." It's simple, and it avoids confusion. For Next Style, for this page style I use "Default Page Style" as the Next Style.

There is nothing else to be set on this tab. Leave the Category field set for "Custom Style."

Page

The Page parameters will be the same for the title page as for the half title pages.

- Paper Format: Enter the dimensions for the trim size selected for the book (5" x 8", 6" x 9", etc.), and be sure the Orientation is set for Portrait. Leave Text Direction set for "Left-to-right" (the default) unless the book is in a language that is written and read right-to-left (such as, for example, Arabic and Hebrew).
- Margins: Enter the margin dimensions decided on for the body text of the book (ignoring headers and footers, since the title page doesn't have a header or a footer).
- Layout Settings: A title page is always a right-hand page, so for Page Layout choose "Only Right." A title page doesn't display a page number, so ignore the field for Page Numbers. Leave the Gutter Position field set to the default of "Left."

Area

This this tab is for setting a background color, texture/pattern, or image that will cover the entire area of all page designated with this page style. For most books it is not used. Leave the "None" options box at the top selected.

Transparency

Unless a background color has been selected, this tab is not used. When a background color, pattern, or image has been selected, this tab allows adjusting the transparency of the background color, pattern, or image. For most books, this setting will not be used.

Header

A title page does not display a header. Leave the box for "Header On" unchecked.

Footer

A title page does not display a footer. Leave the box for "Footer On" unchecked.

Border

Most books won't use a border, so nothing on this tab needs to be changed. The appearance of a book can be enhanced by placing borders on some or all pages. If a border is desired, this tab allows specifying all the parameters of a page border, as described beginning on page 31, above.

Columns

The Columns tab in the Page Style settings dialogue box affects the entire area of each page using the page style being created or edited. A title page only has one column. Do not change anything on this tab.

Footnote

Footnotes will never appear on a title page. Do not change anything on this tab.

Text Grid

Ignore this tab.

Copyright Page

The copyright page is always a left-hand page, the obverse side of the title page. As a left-hand page, some settings are unique. The copyright page style has to be created as a new style, using the following settings:

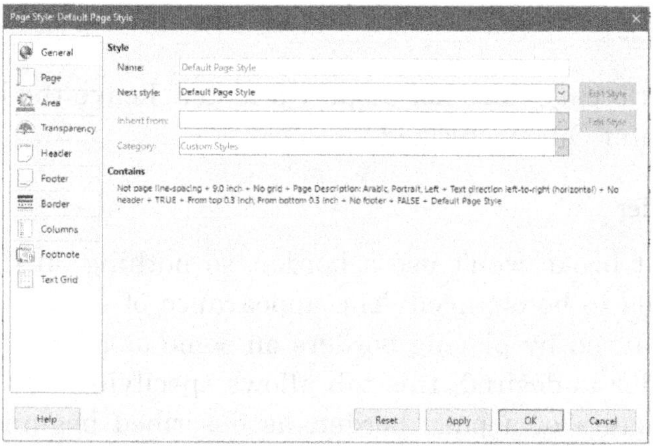

General

I use the "Default Page Style" for the copyright page, with a few changes to other tabs. Under this tab, do not make any changes.

Page

The copyright page does not display a header, footer, or page number. Fill in the page size and margin dimensions the same as for the half title and title pages.

Area

Unless you want to use a background color, pattern, or image on the copyright page, ignore this tab.

Transparency

Unless you want to use a background color, pattern, or image on the copyright page, ignore this tab.

Header

The copyright page does not display a header. Leave the box for "Header On" unchecked.

Footer

The copyright page does not display a footer. Leave the box for "Footer On" unchecked.

Border

If you want a border on the copyright page, the parameters are explained beginning on page 31.

Columns

The Columns tab in the Page Style settings dialogue box affects the entire area of each page using the page style being created or edited. The copyright page only has one column. Do not change anything on this tab.

Footnote

Footnotes will never appear on the copyright page. Do not change anything on this tab.

Text Grid

Ignore this tab.

Front Matter First Page

The "Front Matter" essentially consists of everything that comes before the main body of a book. Depending on the type of book, how many people the author wants to recognize, and what their contributions may have been, the front matter may consist of one or two sections or it may be a half dozen or more. How many sections to include (and whether or not to include them at all) is completely up to the author's discretion. Even the order in which sections of the front matter are arranged isn't consistent from one "expert" to another. Front matter may include the following sections:

- Dedication
- Epigraph
- Table of Contents
- Foreword
- Preface
- Acknowledgments
- Introduction (may be in the front matter, or may be treated as the first chapter of the book body)

A dedication and an epigraph, if used, probably won't be more than one page in length. Other sections of the front matter may require more than one page. For this reason, page styles for front matter are generally the same as page styles for the book body, with a couple of exceptions:

- Front matter pages after the copyright page should display page numbers, but the page numbers are formatted using lower case Roman numerals. This means that, like the book body, there has to be a separate page style created for the first page of each section of front matter, and then there have to be definitions created for the left-hand and right-hand pages of the front matter.
- Some authors do not use headers on any front matter pages. That allows creating a single page style that covers both the left-hand and right-hand page styles. If you intend to use headers, with left-hand pages displaying a different header than right-hand pages, then separate page styles will be needed for left-hand front matter and right-hand front matter. (For simplicity, my template does not display headers on front matter pages.)

In my template, I named the first page of front mater sections “First Page – Front Matter.” There must also be a first page from the book body, so it important to keep them separate to avoid formatting problems. The settings are:

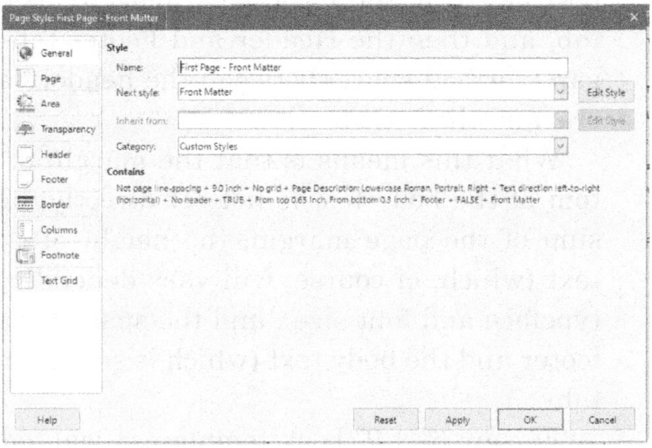

General

- Style: Enter "First Page – Front Matter" in the field for Name, and enter "Front Matter" in the field for Next Style. [Note: If there will be headers on the front matter pages, then make the Next Style "Left Page – Front Matter.")

Page

- Page Format: As for the preceding page styles, the page width and height should be set to the trim size decided upon for the book, and the page orientation should be set (usually to Portrait).
- Margins: Margins work differently in Writer than they do in Microsoft Word. In Word, there is a setting for the margins for the text body, and that remains the same whether or not there are headers or footers. The margin between the top or bottom of a page and a header or footer is set separately, and function independently of the margins for the body test.

  Headers and footers in LibreOffice Writer are positioned by the basic page margins set on this tab, and then the Header and Footer tabs set the gap (vertical space) between the headers and footers, and the body text.

  What this means is that the margin to the bottom of the body test is not set directly, but is the sum of the page margin, the height of the footer text (which, of course, will vary depending on the typeface and font size), and the space between the footer and the body text (which is set on the Footer tab).

  For my 6" x 9" book template, I wanted the top and bottom margins for the body text to be approximately ⅝", or 0.625". I rounded this to 0.65" and used that setting for the top and bottom margins of pages with no headers and no footers. BUT ... for a page that will display a footer, the bottom margin has to be changed. The footer should be approximately halfway between the edge of the page and the bottom of the body text, so I used a dimension of 0.30". For a book with top and bottom margins of ½", a page margin of 0.20" might be about right for pages with footers.

- Layout Settings: The first page of any front matter section (except the copyright page) is always a right-hand page, so the Page Layout field needs to be set to "Only Right." Front matter pages display a page number in the bottom margin, so the page number field needs to be changed to lower case Roman numerals (i, ii, iii, ...). Leave Gutter Position set for "Left."

Area

Unless you want to use a background color, pattern, or image on all front matter first pages, ignore this tab.

Transparency

Unless you want to use a background color, pattern, or image on all front matter first pages, ignore this tab.

Header

As with chapter first pages in the book body, the first page of each front matter section should not display a header. Leave the "Header on" box on this tab unchecked.

Footer

Check the box for "Footer on." Leave the Left margin and Right margin set to 0.00". Set Spacing to 0.20" and set Height to 0.20".

Border

Unless you want a border on the first page of every front matter section, skip this tab. If you want a border, the parameters are explained beginning on page 31.

Columns

The Columns tab in the Page Style settings dialogue box affects the entire area of each page using the page style being created or edited. There is no reason for the first page of any section of the front matter to be in multiple columns. Skip this tab

Footnote

Footnotes in front matter are extremely unusual. Unless there is a need for footnotes, skip this tab.

Text Grid

Ignore this tab.

Front Matter Continuation Pages

Some sections of the front matter (such as an epigraph) always occupy only a single page, but others may occupy two or more pages. Just like the book body, continuation pages of front matter sections occupy the full page and are formatted as mirrored left-hand and right-hand pages. If you choose not to display headers in the front matter, the following settings should work.

If you want to display alternating left and right headers in the front matter the same as in the book body, separate page styles will have to be created for left front matter page and right front matter page. For those settings, jump forward to the section on editing the built-in Left Page and Right Page styles. The only difference between left-hand and right-hand front matter pages and left-hand and right-hand book body pages will be that the page number format for front matter pages will be lower case Roman numerals.

The following settings are for left-hand and right-hand front matter pages without headers:

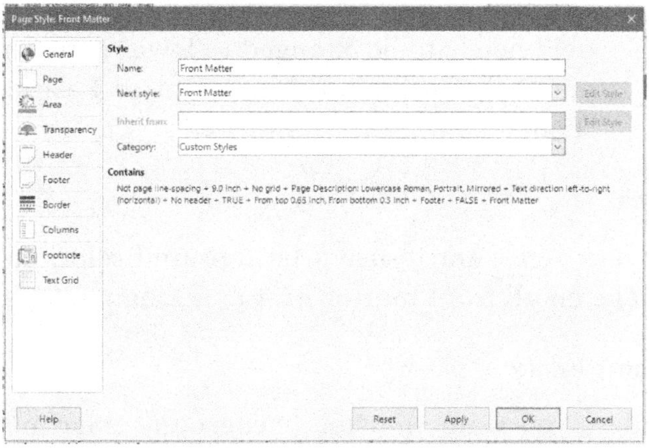

General

- Style: Enter "Front Matter" in the field for Name, and enter "Front Matter" in the field for Next Style. [Note: If there will be headers on the front matter pages, then make the Next Style "Right Page – Front Matter.")

Page

- Page Format: As for the preceding page styles, the page width and height should be set to the trim size decided upon for the book, and the page orientation should be set (usually to Portrait).

- Margins: Set the Left, Right, Top, and Gutter dimensions the same as for all the preceding pages. For the Bottom margin, enter the same dimension used for the "First Page – Front Matter" style.
- Layout Settings: Any section of front matter that extends beyond one page is formatted just like the body of the book, with alternating left-hand and right-hand pages. Change the Page Layout field to "Mirrored." Front matter pages display a page number in the bottom margin, so the page number field needs to be changed to lower case Roman numerals (i, ii, iii, ...). Leave Gutter Position set for "Left."

Area

Unless you want to use a background color, pattern, or image on all front matter first pages, ignore this tab.

Transparency

Unless you want to use a background color, pattern, or image on all front matter first pages, ignore this tab.

Header

Whether or not to include headers on the continuation pages of front matter sections is entirely optional. I have published books with headers on front matter pages, and I have published other books without headers on front matter pages. It's easier to omit them, in which case leave the "Header on" box on this tab unchecked. [To display headers on front matter continuation pages, create two new page styles, one for "Front Matter – Left Page" and one for "Front Matter – Right Page." Use the settings described for the built-in Left Page and Right Page styles.

Footer

Check the box for "Footer on." Leave the Left margin and Right margin set to 0.00". Set Spacing to 0.20" and set Height to 0.20".

Border

Unless you want a border on the first page of every front matter section, skip this tab. If you want a border, the parameters are explained beginning on page 31.

Columns

The Columns tab in the Page Style settings dialogue box affects the entire area of each page using the page style being created or edited. There is no reason for the front matter to be in multiple columns. Skip this tab

Footnote

Footnotes in front matter are extremely unusual. Unless there is a need for footnotes, skip this tab.

Text Grid

Ignore this tab.

First Page

The "First Page" style is one of the built-in page styles that is pre-defined in Writer, but the default settings for most parameters need to be edited to properly format a book for print. This is the style that will be assigned to the first page of every chapter in the book, so it is important to get this right. To edit the settings, right click on "First Page" in the page style menu of the LibreOffice Writer sidebar, then click "Edit Style."

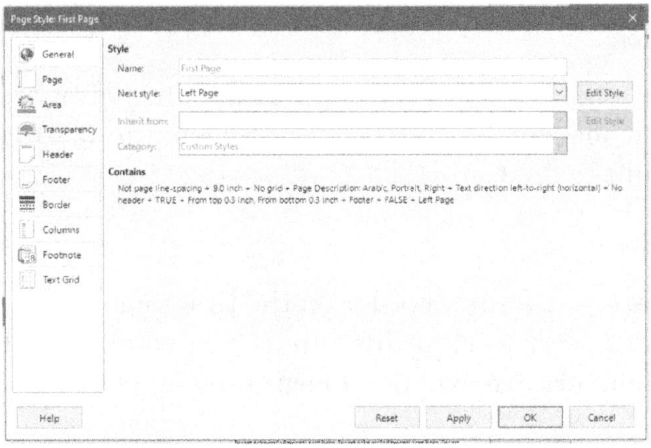

General

- Style: Because this is a pre-defined style, the style name ("First Page") is already entered, and cannot be changed. The Next Style field should already be filled in with "Left Page." If it is not, change it to "Left Page."

Page

- Page Format: As for the preceding page styles, the page width and height should be set to the trim size decided upon for the book, and the page orientation should be set (usually to Portrait).
- Margins: Set the Left, Right, Top, and Gutter dimensions the same as for all the preceding pages. Higher-quality books always have new chapters begin on a right-hand (odd-numbered) page, with a page number but no header. This means that, even when body pages incorporate the page numbers into the headers, for the first page of each chapter the page number is placed in a footer. This means

the Bottom margin must be set to the same dimension used for the Bottom margin in the "Front Matter – First Page." For the Bottom margin, enter the same dimension used for the "First Page – Front Matter" style.

- Layout Settings: The first page of any new chapter is always a right-hand page, so the Page Layout field needs to be set to "Only Right." First pages display a page number in the bottom margin and, for the book body, page numbers should be set in Arabic numerals. This is the default setting in Writer, but be sure "Page Numbers" correctly indicates Arabic numerals.

  Writer handles page numbering very differently from Microsoft Word. Readers familiar with Word probably know that when starting a new section, the page numbering can be changed in the "Page Number Format" dialogue box, where a new starting number can be entered. LibreOffice Writer counts every page from the beginning of the document, and to display any number other than the actual page number an "offset" must be entered into a separate dialogue box that is opened by highlighting the page number in the footer, right clicking the page number, and selecting "Edit Fields."

  The offset field will default to showing zero. Enter a negative value (such as "-5") and check to see if the page number displayed is correct. If not, repeat the process until the page number displays "1".

  Leave Gutter Position set for "Left."

Area

Unless you want to use a background color, pattern, or image on all front matter first pages, ignore this tab.

Transparency

Unless you want to use a background color, pattern, or image on all front matter first pages, ignore this tab.

Header

The first page of each new chapter should not display a header. Leave the "Header on" box on this tab unchecked.

Footer

Check the box for "Footer on." Leave the Left margin and Right margin set to 0.00". Set Spacing to 0.20" and set Height to 0.20".

Border

Unless you want a border on the first page of every new chapter, skip this tab. If you want a border, the parameters are explained beginning on page 31.

Columns

The Columns tab in the Page Style settings dialogue box affects the entire area of each page using the page style being created or edited. Unless there is a reason to format an entire book in multiple columns, skip this tab

Footnote

Footnotes in front matter are unusual in fiction, but commonplace in non-fiction. Unless there is a need for footnotes, skip this tab. This tab has default parameters predefined, so for a few brief footnotes nothing needs to be changes. If longer footnotes are split and extend onto the next page, it may be necessary to go to the "Footnote Area" parameter, check the choice for "Maximum footnote height," and change the setting from the pre-defined 1.00" to a larger number.

Text Grid

Ignore this tab.

Left Page

The Left Page style is one of the built-in page styles that is pre-defined in Writer, but the default settings for most parameters need to be edited to properly format a book for print. This is the style that will be assigned to every left-hand (even-numbered) page of every chapter in the book, so it is important to get this right. To edit the settings, right click on "Left Page" in the page style menu of the LibreOffice Writer sidebar, then click "Edit Style."

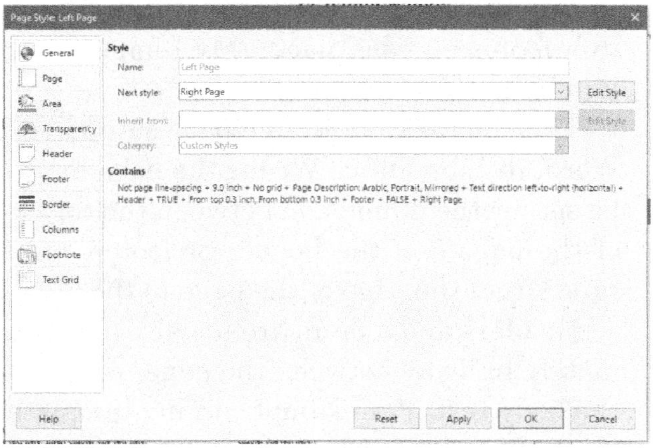

General

- Style: Because this is a pre-defined style, the style name ("Left Page") is already entered, and cannot be changed. The Next Style field should already be filled in with "Right Page." If it is not, change it to "Right Page."

Page

- Page Format: As for the preceding page styles, the page width and height should be set to the trim size decided upon for the book, and the page orientation should be set (usually to Portrait).
- Margins: Set the Left, Right, and Gutter dimensions the same as for all the preceding pages. Book body pages usually have alternating headers, for example displaying the author's name in the header of left-hand pages and the title of the book in the header of right-hand pages. Some authors and book designers prefer to incorporate page numbering into the headers; others place page numbers in a footer on each page. (My template puts page numbers in footers.)

  This means that, unlike page setup in Microsoft Word, in LibreOffice Writer the page margin must be set for the dimension between the top or bottom of the page and the header or footer, *not* the distance from the edge of the page to the body text.

  Headers and footers are usually placed approximately halfway between the edges of the page and the body text. For example, in my template I want the body test margin to be 0.65" from the top and bottom edges of the pages. For pages with headers, I set the top margin at 0.30"; spacing between the header and the body text is controlled by the settings in the "Header" tab. If the desired top margin is approximately ½ inch, try a top margin of 0.20" for pages that will have headers.

  The Bottom margin must be set to the same dimension used for the Bottom margin in the "Front Matter – First Page." For the Bottom margin, enter the same dimension used for the "First Page – Front Matter" style.

- Layout Settings: The left-hand pages of any chapter are always (obviously) left-hand pages and the side margins and gutter are mirrored between left-hand and right-hand pages, so the Page Layout field needs to be set to "Mirrored." Left-hand body pages display page numbers in Arabic numerals. This is the default setting in Writer, but be sure "Page Numbers" correctly indicates Arabic numerals.

  Writer handles page numbering very differently from Microsoft Word. Readers familiar with Word probably know that when starting a new section, the page numbering can be changed in the "Page Number Format" dialogue box, where a new starting number can be entered. LibreOffice Writer counts every page from the beginning of the document, and to display any number other than the actual page number an "offset" must be entered into a separate dialogue box that is opened by highlighting the page number in the footer, right clicking the page number, and selecting "Edit Fields."

  The offset field will default to showing zero. Enter the same offset that was determined when formatting the "First Page" style.

  Leave Gutter Position set for "Left."

Area

Unless you want to use a background color, pattern, or image on all front matter first pages, ignore this tab.

Transparency

Unless you want to use a background color, pattern, or image on all front matter first pages, ignore this tab.

Header

Check the box for “Header on.” Leave the Left margin and Right margin set to 0.00”. Set Spacing to 0.20” and set Height to 0.20”.

Footer

Check the box for “Footer on.” Leave the Left margin and Right margin set to 0.00”. Set Spacing to 0.20” and set Height to 0.20”.

Border

Unless you want a border on every left-hand page of every chapter, skip this tab. If you want a border, the parameters are explained beginning on page 31.

Columns

The Columns tab in the Page Style settings dialogue box affects the entire area of each page using the page style being created or edited. Unless there is a reason to format an entire book in multiple columns, skip this tab

Footnote

Enter the same settings that were used on the “First Page” style. In most cases, the pre-defined default settings are probably adequate and do not need to be changed.

Text Grid

Ignore this tab.

Right Page

The Right Page style is another page style that is pre-defined in Writer, and which needs to be edited to properly format a book for print. This style is assigned to every right-hand (odd-numbered) page of every chapter in the book *except* for the first page of each new chapter. To edit the settings, right click on "Right Page" in the page style menu of the LibreOffice Writer sidebar, then click "Edit Style."

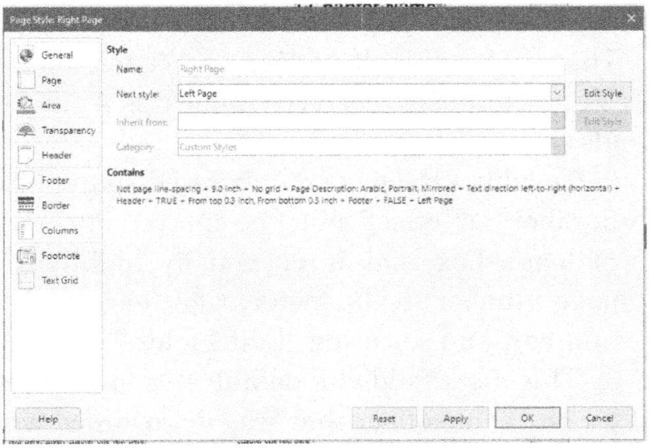

General

- Style: Because this is a pre-defined style, the style name ("Right Page") is already entered, and cannot be changed. The Next Style field should already be filled in with "Left Page." If it is not, change it to "Left Page."

Page

- Page Format: As for the preceding page styles, the page width and height should be set to the trim size decided upon for the book, and the page orientation should be set (usually to Portrait).

- Margins: Set the Left, Right, and Gutter dimensions the same as for all the preceding pages. Set the Top and Bottom margins to the exact same dimensions used on the "Left Page" style.
- Layout Settings: The right-hand pages of any chapter are always (obviously) right-hand pages and the side margins and gutter are mirrored between left-hand and right-hand pages, so the Page Layout field needs to be set to "Mirrored." Left-hand body pages display page numbers in Arabic numerals. This is the default setting in Writer, but be sure "Page Numbers" correctly indicates Arabic numerals.

  To adjust the page number to display the correct number, an "offset" must be entered into a separate dialogue box that is opened by highlighting the page number in the footer, right clicking the page number, and selecting "Edit Fields."

  The offset field will default to showing zero. Enter the same offset that was determined when formatting the "First Page" style.

  - Page line-spacing printing is particularly useful for documents that will have two pages set next to each other (for example, in a book or brochure), for multi-column layouts, and for documents intended for double-sided printing. If you wish to try this feature, activate it by clicking on the checkbox. All paragraphs that have Page line-spacing activated will use that line distance, aligning the bottom of a text line to the next grid line, regardless of font size or presence of graphics.

Leave Gutter Position set for "Left."

Area

Unless you want to use a background color, pattern, or image on all front matter first pages, ignore this tab.

Transparency

Unless you want to use a background color, pattern, or image on all front matter first pages, ignore this tab.

Header

Check the box for "Header on." Leave the Left margin and Right margin set to 0.00". Set Spacing to 0.20" and set Height to 0.20".

Footer

Check the box for "Footer on." Leave the Left margin and Right margin set to 0.00". Set Spacing to 0.20" and set Height to 0.20".

Border

Unless you want a border on every left-hand page of every chapter, skip this tab. If you want a border, the parameters are explained beginning on page 31.

Columns

The Columns tab in the Page Style settings dialogue box affects the entire area of each page using the page style being created or edited. Unless there is a reason to format an entire book in multiple columns, skip this tab

Footnote

Enter the same settings that were used on the "First Page" style. In most cases, the pre-defined default settings are probably adequate and do not need to be changed.

Text Grid

Ignore this tab.

Starting New Chapters or Sections

To reiterate: LibreOffice Writer does *not* work the same as Microsoft Word. Readers making the transition from Word to Writer *must* be aware of some major differences, and must adapt their work habits accordingly. One of the things that has to be changed is the way transitions to new chapters (and new sections of front matter or back matter) are handled.

Many users of Microsoft Word, even many long-time users, persist in using a simple page break (created by typing CTRL+Enter) to make a break to a new chapter. Although this works for raw manuscripts and even for e-Books, it does *not* work for printed books. The correct way to create chapter breaks in Word is to insert a section break, either a "Next page" break if it's not important for new chapters to begin on right-hand pages, or "Odd page" if it is important for new chapters to always occur on right-hand pages.

Neither of these methods works in LibreOffice Writer. In Writer, pressing CTRL+Enter does jump to a new page, BUT that new page can't be set to the "First Page" style to begin a new chapter. Instead, to start a new chapter go to the "Insert tab in the menu bar at the top of the screen, and select "Manual Break." This will open a dialogue box.

Select "Page break." Then click the arrow at the right-hand end of the "Page Style" field, and select the page style the new page should be (such as "First Page" for new chapters in the body of the book).

5 — Book Body Format

Paragraph Format

After page styles, paragraph styles control the appearance of the printed pages and can make the difference between a hack job and a professional-looking publication. As in Word, paragraphs can be styled and changed individually but, for a book, the preferred way to handle this is to modify or to create paragraph styles. The easiest way to change all the text in a book, whether changing the typeface, the font size, the justification, or all, is to edit the applicable paragraph style. This automatically applies the changes globally, through the full length of the document.

The body text in a printed book should be set as fully justified, which means that the spacing of the words on each line is adjusted so the right edge on the block of text forms a vertical line just like the left edge. In proper terminology, text is "right justified," "left justified," "fully justified (both edges align), or "center justified." Most word processors just call it "justified" when referring to fully-justified.

The difference in appearance between left-justified text (which is also referred to as "ragged right") and fully-justified text is significant. Printing a book (and even releasing an e-book) with left-justified text looks extremely unfinished. The simple step of setting the body text styles to justified makes a huge difference in how professional a book looks.

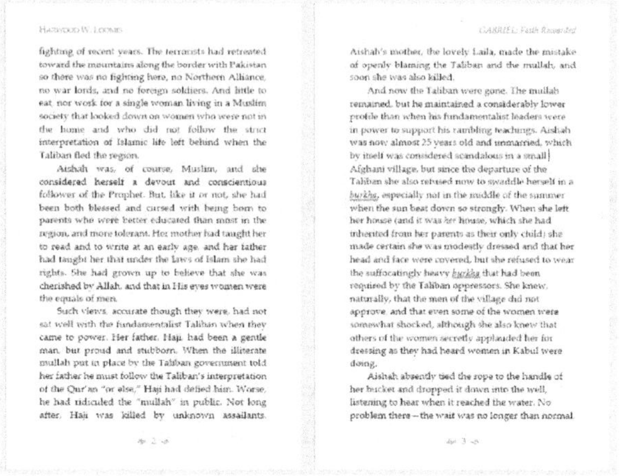

HARWOOD W. LOOMIS

fighting of recent years. The terrorists had retreated toward the mountains along the border with Pakistan so there was no fighting here, no Northern Alliance, no war lords, and no foreign soldiers. And little to eat, nor work for a single woman living in a Muslim society that looked down on women who were not in the home and who did not follow the strict interpretation of Islamic life left behind when the Taliban fled the region.

Aishah was, of course, Muslim, and she considered herself a devout and conscientious follower of the Prophet. But, like it or not, she had been both blessed and cursed with being born to parents who were better educated than most in the region, and more tolerant. Her mother had taught her to read and to write at an early age, and her father had taught her that under the laws of Islam she had rights. She had grown up to believe that she was cherished by Allah, and that in His eyes women were the equals of men.

Such views, accurate though they were, had not sat well with the fundamentalist Taliban when they came to power. Her father, Haji, had been a gentle man, but proud and stubborn. When the illiterate mullah put in place by the Taliban government told her father he must follow the Taliban's interpretation of the Qur'an "or else," Haji had defied him. Worse, he had ridiculed the "mullah" in public. Not long after, Haji was killed by unknown assailants.

2

GABRIEL: Faith Rewarded

Aishah's mother, the lovely Laila, made the mistake of openly blaming the Taliban and the mullah, and soon she was also killed.

And now the Taliban were gone. The mullah remained, but he maintained a considerably lower profile than when his fundamentalist leaders were in power to support his rambling teachings. Aishah was now almost 25 years old and unmarried, which by itself was considered scandalous in a small Afghani village, but since the departure of the Taliban she also refused now to swaddle herself in a *burkha*, especially not in the middle of the summer when the sun beat down so strongly. When she left her house (and it was *her* house, which she had inherited from her parents as their only child) she made certain she was modestly dressed and that her head and face were covered, but she refused to wear the suffocatingly heavy *burkha* that had been required by the Taliban oppressors. She knew, naturally, that the men of the village did not approve, and that even some of the women were somewhat shocked, although she also knew that others of the women secretly applauded her for dressing as they had heard women in Kabul were doing.

Aishah absently tied the rope to the handle of her bucket and dropped it down into the well, listening to hear when it reached the water. No problem there—the wait was no longer than normal.

3

In the sample above, the left page is fully justified, the right page is "ragged right"

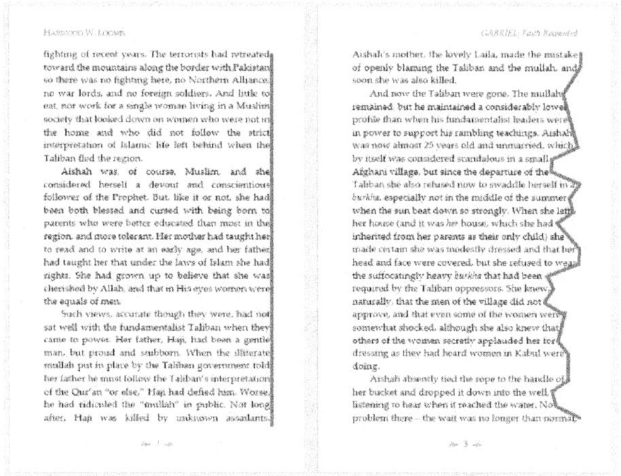

HARWOOD W. LOOMIS

fighting of recent years. The terrorists had retreated toward the mountains along the border with Pakistan so there was no fighting here, no Northern Alliance, no war lords, and no foreign soldiers. And little to eat, nor work for a single woman living in a Muslim society that looked down on women who were not in the home and who did not follow the strict interpretation of Islamic life left behind when the Taliban fled the region.

Aishah was, of course, Muslim, and she considered herself a devout and conscientious follower of the Prophet. But, like it or not, she had been both blessed and cursed with being born to parents who were better educated than most in the region, and more tolerant. Her mother had taught her to read and to write at an early age, and her father had taught her that under the laws of Islam she had rights. She had grown up to believe that she was cherished by Allah, and that in His eyes women were the equals of men.

Such views, accurate though they were, had not sat well with the fundamentalist Taliban when they came to power. Her father, Haji, had been a gentle man, but proud and stubborn. When the illiterate mullah put in place by the Taliban government told her father he must follow the Taliban's interpretation of the Qur'an "or else," Haji had defied him. Worse, he had ridiculed the "mullah" in public. Not long after, Haji was killed by unknown assailants.

GABRIEL: Faith Rewarded

Aishah's mother, the lovely Laila, made the mistake of openly blaming the Taliban and the mullah, and soon she was also killed.

And now the Taliban were gone. The mullah remained, but he maintained a considerably lower profile than when his fundamentalist leaders were in power to support his rambling teachings. Aishah was now almost 25 years old and unmarried, which by itself was considered scandalous in a small Afghani village, but since the departure of the Taliban she also refused now to swaddle herself in a *burkha*, especially not in the middle of the summer when the sun beat down so strongly. When she left her house (and it was *her* house, which she had inherited from her parents as their only child) she made certain she was modestly dressed and that her head and face were covered, but she refused to wear the suffocatingly heavy *burkha* that had been required by the Taliban oppressors. She knew, naturally, that the men of the village did not approve, and that even some of the women were somewhat shocked, although she also knew that others of the women secretly applauded her for dressing as they had heard women in Kabul were doing.

Aishah absently tied the rope to the handle of her bucket and dropped it down into the well, listening to hear when it reached the water. No problem there—the wait was no longer than normal.

3

Fully-justified text looks neat. Left justified text looks "ragged," hence the name.

The visual impact of justified text compared to "ragged right" is immediately obvious, and it says a lot about the quality of the book. It's an immediate clue as to whether a book was published by an amateur or by a professional who cares about his or her creation.

Paragraph Styles

Writer includes a number of pre-defined paragraph styles, each of which can be edited for use in a book. The paragraph style that should be assigned to the body text for a book is the built-in style named (cleverly) "Default Paragraph Style." This chapter will review and explain the paragraph style settings that are most likely to require adjustments for use in a printed book, using the "Default Paragraph Style" as the example. Other paragraph styles can be edited according to the author's preferences, and new styles can be created where necessary.

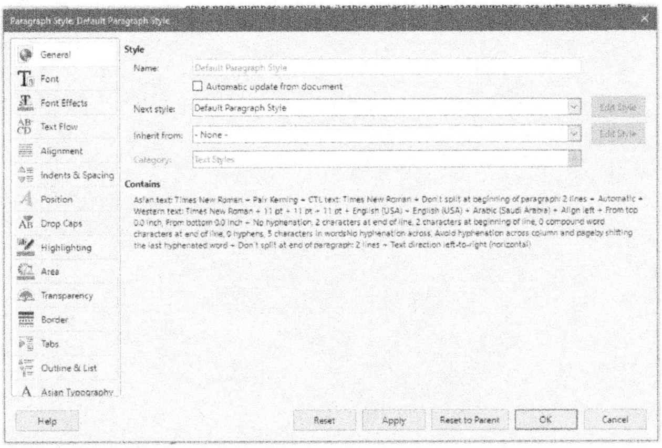

As for editing and creating page styles, first ensure that the sidebar is visible, and click on the Paragraph Styles icon at the upper left of the sidebar to display a list of the paragraph styled defined for the document. Then right click the style to be edited and select "Edit Style" (or "New" to create a new paragraph style).

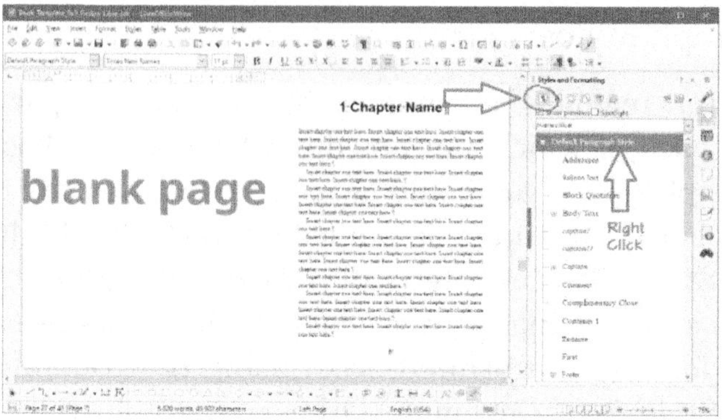

This will open the paragraph styles dialogue window, where all the parameters for a paragraph style are set:

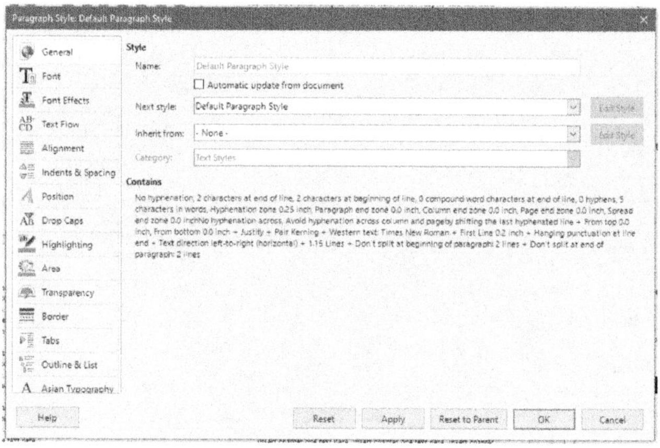

General

- Style: Because this is a pre-defined style, the style name ("Default Paragraph Style") is already entered, and cannot be changed. The Next Style field should already be filled in with "Default Paragraph Style." This is correct for body text paragraphs. This would also be correct for a custom style used as the first (opening) paragraph for new chapters. An opening paragraph with no first line indent or with a fancy drop cap would be followed by a standard ("Default Paragraph Style") paragraph.

Font

This tab displays two sub-tabs, one for Western and one for eastern typography. Since this book is written for authors writing in English and western languages, the following will only discuss the setting for the "Western" tab.

- Font: This setting selects the typeface to be used for the paragraph style (such as Times New Roman, or Arial). It will initially be set for whatever font and type size have been set globally for Writer in Tools > Options. If a different typeface or size is selected here, this setting will override the default *for the current document.*
- Style: All fonts can be set to Regular (Upright), Bold, Italic, or Bold Italic. For the default body text style, leave this set to Regular. For paragraph styles for such things as headers, this may be changed to Bold, Italic, or Bold Italic, as desired.
- Size: Like the typeface, the type size will initially be set to the default sent in Writer's Tools > Options settings. If a different typeface or size is selected here, this setting will override the default *for the current document*. The drop-down menu allows selecting the type size only by whole numbers and, above 14-point, it begins skipping numbers. Both TrueType and OpenType fonts can be set to sizes of one-half point, so it is possible to type in a type size of, for example, 9.5-point or 13.5-point.
- Language: This field should indicate the language that was set when you installed LibreOffice. It can be changed here if the book is written in a different language; otherwise, do not change it.

Font Effects

- Font Color: This setting changes the color of every character in every paragraph of the style. Since books are usually printed with black text, for the "Default Paragraph Style" leave the text color set to "Automatic." If the book is going to be printed in color and you want to set special paragraph styles (such as chapter titles, for example) in color, that color is selected here.
- Text Decoration: The fields in this section also affect all text in every paragraph using the style being edited. These settings control overlining, strikethrough, and underling. It is best to leave these set to the default "Without" in paragraph styles, and apply these attributes to selected words or phrases individually throughout the manuscript.
- Effects: The fields in this section also affect all text in every paragraph using the style being edited. These settings control case (upper case, lower case, capitalizing each word, and small caps. It is best to leave these set to the default "Without" in paragraph styles, and apply these attributes to selected words or phrases individually throughout the manuscript.

Text Flow

- Hyphenation: LibreOffice Writer's default setting to for automatic hyphenation to be turned off. Especially in manuscripts formatted for smaller pages and using long words, this can result in many lines of text with large and unequal spacing between words because of justification. Turning on hyphenation by clicking the check box for

"Automatically" solves that by hyphenating multi-syllabic words when they occur at the end of a line.

When hyphenation is turned on, several options become available to customize how hyphenation will function. For example, the default allows hyphenation to leave syllables of just two characters at the end and the beginning of lines. If that's difficult to read, try increasing both to three or four characters.

- Hyphenation Across: This group of settings becomes available only in automatic hyphenation is turned on. When using automatic hyphenation, I recommend not changing the settings for "Characters at line end," "Characters at Line begin," and "Compound characters at line end;" leave these set to the default value of two.

  The next field in this section is "Maximum consecutive hyphenated lines." The default value for this is zero. Leaving this at zero potentially allows numerous consecutive lines to end in hyphens, which is not good book design. I recommend changing this to two (2).

- Breaks: In Microsoft Word, chapter breaks should be made using section breaks rather than page breaks. LibreOffice Writer uses "sections" very differently from Word, so in Writer a chapter break is made using a page break, and then by assigning a new page style to the first page of the new chapter. This can be automated by using this option. (See page 66).

  This option should not be used for the body text paragraph style ("Default Paragraph Style"). If, for example, paragraph style "Heading 1" is assigned to chapter titles, activating this option by clicking the check box would automatically insert a page break anywhere a paragraph is assigned as style "Heading 1."

This is a useful option, but it is not necessary. I was able to create my book template without using this option.

- Split Options: LibreOffice doesn't seem to use the terms "widows" and "orphans," but this is where widow and orphan control is turned on or off. The default is to have it turned on, as indicated by the check mark on the box "Allow to split paragraph." The default setting is two lines, which is a generally-accepted normal way to format widows and orphans. This can be increased, but increasing the setting can result in some pages with large white spaces at the bottoms because the start of the next paragraph had to be "bumped" to the following page. I recommend leaving this turned on with the default settings of two lines.

Alignment

- Options: This section should probably be named "Justification" to be consistent with most other word processing programs and common terminology. This is where you set the justification for left-justified only, right-justified only, or left- and right-justified. LibreOffice, though, doesn't use the customary terminology. In Writer:
    - "Start" means left (only) justified (ragged right)
    - "Center" means center-aligned (both ends ragged)
    - "End" means right (only) justified (ragged left)
    - "Force Left/Top" means essentially the same as the "Start" setting, except that it affects the

display of paragraphs immediately after a page break. I recommend not using this setting.

    - "Force Right/Bottom" means essentially the same thing as the "End" setting, except that it affects the display of paragraphs immediately after a page break. I recommend not using this setting.
    - "Justified" means both the left-hand and right-hand ends of all lines of text are aligned vertically on their respective margins. This is the preferred setting for printed books.

- Text-to-Text: Leave this field set to "Automatic."
- Properties: Leave text direction set to "Left-to-right (LTR)," unless the book is in a language that reads from right to left (such as Arabic or Hebrew).
- Justification: These fields do not turn full (left and right) justification on or off, but if the "Options" field is set for "Justified" these settings affect how much additional space Writer will insert between words and letters in order to align the text on both margins. I recommend leaving these fields at their default settings, unless your book has numerous lines with too much space between words. If that occurs, try reducing the "Maximum" word spacing field from 133% to 125% or 115%.

Indents & Spacing

This tab is where information is entered regarding whether or not the first line of each paragraph is indented. Standard practice is to indent all paragraphs except the first paragraph following a chapter heading, a major sub-heading, or a scene break. In professional book design the amount by which the first line is indented is an "em," which is a dimension equal to the width of a capital 'M' in the font being used. Word processing programs don't measure paragraph dimensions in ems, they use inches and decimals of an inch (or millimeters, in countries using the metric system). A good number to start with for the first line indentation is .20". Authors may wish to create a new paragraph style, without the first line indent, for opening paragraphs. This new paragraph style could be named, for example, "First Paragraph Style" or "No Indent Style."

For the "Default Paragraph Style" I recommend using the following settings:

- Indent: The fields for "Before text" and 'After text" should be left at zero for the "Default Paragraph Style." For special paragraphs such as quotations that need to stand out, these can be edited to a value of 0.20" or 0.25". For such special paragraphs I prefer to indent both sides by the same value. For the "Default Paragraph Style" the first line of each paragraph should be indented. I use a value of 0.20". Depending on the typeface, type size, and page size of the book, if 0.20" is not sufficient, this value can be increased to 0.25" or 0.33". A value of 0.50" (½") is excessive.
- Spacing: The values entered in this section affect the appearance and readability of the book. Some authors and some book designers prefer to add extra space between paragraphs. While this practice seems to be prevalent in e-Books, this is virtually never found in printed books from professional publishers. Unless there is a very good reason for doing this, I recommend leaving both these fields set at the default value of zero.

  For certain special paragraph types, however, these fields should be changed. For example, chapter titles should be assigned to the "Heading 1" paragraph style. For most books, the chapter title should be positioned between one-quarter and one-third of the way down the page. Rather than typing in a series of paragraph breaks to create empty space on the page, the correct approach is to edit these fields for the "Heading 1" paragraph style. Entering a value of 2.00" for the "Above paragraph" field and a value of 0.33" for the "After paragraph" field is a good starting point. These values can always be changed to tweak the final appearance of the book.

- Line Spacing: Like most word processors, LibreOffice Writer defaults to single line spacing. Depending on what font is selected for the printed version, single spacing may be acceptable. However, professional book designers usually prefer to add a bit of extra space between lines to open up the text so the pages don't look too dense. In LibreOffice Writer, this is set from the "Spacing" section in the Page Style dialogue window.

  At the bottom of the Paragraph Style box there is a place to set "Line spacing." The choices offered are "Single," "1.15 lines," "1.50 lines," "Double," "Proportional," "At least," "Leading," and "Fixed."

  - "Single" is self-explanatory. This is default single-spaced lines, with the vertical space between lines controlled by the metrics of the font selected.
  - "1.15 lines" adds 15 percent to the default vertical spacing between lines. This is often a good choice for most fonts and is generally a safe starting point. If this setting doesn't look right for the particular type face and font size selected, then one of the following options may be needed.

- "1.50 lines" is simply one and one-half line spacing. While this may be useful in some applications or situations, it is not used for either book manuscripts or formatting for print.
- "Double": Traditional double spacing, equivalent to adding a second line break ("Enter" stroke) between lines. This is the default setting for book manuscripts to be sent to agents or to publishers, but should not be used in formatting a book for print.
- "Proportional": This field allows entering a spacing based on a percentage of the single space dimension. This can be adjusted in increments of one percent, which would allow a setting of 105% (1.05 line spacing) or 110% (1.10 line spacing).
- "At least": If you use different font sizes within a paragraph, the line spacing is automatically adjusted to the largest font size. If you prefer to have identical spacing for all lines, specify a value in At least that corresponds to the largest font size.
- "Leading": This field corresponds to the traditional typesetting practice of inserting narrow strips of lead between lines of type to control vertical spacing. In print terminology this is usually expressed in terms such as "11-point type on 13-point leading." This is not based on a proportion or percentage, it adds a specific number of points to the space between lines.
- "Fixed": Sets the line spacing to exactly match the value that you enter in the box. This can result in cropped characters if the line height is set to a value smaller than what the font size requires.

- Activate page line-spacing: Page line-spacing printing is particularly useful for documents that will have two pages set next to each other (for example, in a book or brochure), for multi-column layouts, and for documents intended for double-sided printing. If page line-spacing has been activated from the "Page Styles" settings, this checkbox should display a check mark. UNcheck the box if for any reason you wish to exempt a specific paragraph style from page line-spacing. In general, if you are using page line-spacing, it is best to leave this field checked.

Position

This tab controls certain attributes of all text in the paragraph style. Do not change anything on this tab.

Drop Caps

Drop caps (enlarged capital letters at the beginning of paragraphs) are a stylistic feature that can be used to enhance the appearance of books. Like most modern word processing software, LibreOffice Writer includes a feature to create drop caps, and to assign a drop cap to a paragraph style so that every paragraph in that style will automatically display a drop cap at the beginning of the paragraph.

Drop caps should not be configured for the "Default Paragraph Style." If used, drop caps should only be used to begin the first sentence of new chapters. To do this automatically using paragraph styles, create a new paragraph and name it something like "Chapter First Paragraph," something that will be unique to just those paragraphs. Most of the other setting will be the same as for the "Default Paragraph Style, but the "Drop Caps" settings will be used.

- Settings:
  - Click on the checkbox for "Display drop caps" to activate drop caps. This will make the other attribute fields available for editing.
  - "Whole word": Typically, drop caps are used only for the first letter of a new chapter. Clicking on this checkbox will result in the entire first word being set in drop caps. Try this and see if you like it, but be careful. Just because Writer offers this option doesn't mean that using it is a good idea.
  - "Number of characters": The default entry in this field, "1," applies the drop cap style to only the first letter of the first word of the paragraph. This field can be used to increase that to two letters, three letters, or any number of letters.
  - "Lines": This field sets the height of the drop cap to a specified number of text lines. The default is three lines, which seems to be the default for many word processing programs ("apps"). Three is a good setting, but you might try two and see if you prefer that. I don't recommend setting drop caps to more than three lines in height.
  - "Space to text": This field controls the amount of horizontal space between a drop cap letter and the body text that follows it. The default setting is 0.00 inches, which may be adequate. If the drop caps in your chapters all look a bit cramped, this setting can be adjusted in increments of two one-hundredths of an inch (0.02"). Be careful not to make this distance too large,

or the drop cap characters may appear to be lost or stranded on the page.

- Contents: Do not change either of these fields.

Highlighting

- Leave this setting at "None." Clicking on a color will result in adding a background color to every line of text using the paragraph style.

Area

- Leave this setting at "None." Clicking on a color will result in adding a background color to the entire area of each page with text on it in the paragraph style.

Transparency

- Area transparency mode: This entire tab only applies if a background color or pattern has been selected on the "Area" tab. If a background color or pattern has been activated, these settings can be used to modify the appearance of the background.
  - "No transparency": The background color or pattern is full-strength. It remains behind the text, but strong colors or patterns may leave text difficult to read.
  - "Transparency": adjustable from zero (full-intensity) to 100 percent (no color), this field allows adjusting the intensity of a background color or pattern.
  - "Gradient": If the "Gradient" button is clicked, several fields become available to modify a background color or pattern with varying degrees of color saturation on a gradient, and the

set the angle and style of the gradient on the page.

Border

This tab operates similarly to the "Border" tab in the Page Style dialogue window, except that when used here the border falls directly on the edges of the block of text on each page. It also puts a border around any header or footer on the page.

- When applied to the "Default Paragraph Style," this setting also places a border around text on any page styles that are based on the "Default Page Style."

Tabs

As with Microsoft Word, if no tab stops are set the tab spacing defaults to a tab stop every half inch. Using the settings on this tab, tab stops can be configured for any point within the margins, each tab can be set as left-justified, right-justified, centered on the tab, or with a decimal point on the tab. You can also choose to have dots, dashes, or lines preceding tab stops.

Outline & List

Like Microsoft Word, LibreOffice Writer allows the creation of hierarchical bulleted or numbered lists and outlines. The parameters for numbered or bulleted lists can be customized using the settings on this tab.

Asian Typography

These settings apply only when using Asian (Chinese, Japanese, etc.) languages. For books on English and Western languages, skip this tab.

6 — Headers and Footers

Most print books have headers or footers, and usually they have both. What the headers and footers contain is the book designer's choice. If you are self-publishing your own book—you are the book designer. What should go on the tops and bottoms of your pages?

Once again, the best advice is to go to a bookstore (or the books aisle in a Walmart or your local supermarket) and look at actual books in the same genre as your book. What do they put for headers and footers?

There is no requirement for anything other than a page number, and the page number can be located either in the header or in the footer. If the page number is placed in the footer, it is usually placed in the center of the page. Less often, the page number may be located at the outside margin. Don't place your page number on the inside margin—it's too hard to see it there when your reader is trying to find the place where he or she left off.

To give you a head start on your research, I checked a number of books in two genres to see if there was any consistent trend. What I found was that romance novels all seem to handle headers and footers pretty much the same. Looking at history books as examples of non-fiction, I found much less consistency.

In the category of romance novels, I looked at ten titles. Of those, three had the page number centered at the bottom of the page, five had the page number at the outside margin on the top of the page, and two combined the page number and the book's title or author at the outside margin on the top of the page. For the headers, seven had the author's name centered on the even (left-hand) pages and the title centered on the odd (right-hand) pages. One had the title centered at the top of the even pages and the author's name centered at the top of the odd pages. Two combined the page number and author's name at the outside margin of the even pages, and combined the page number and the title at the outside margin of the odd pages.

To make it easy, for general fiction books we can generalize that you won't go wrong to omit a footer (allowing you to reduce the bottom margin), place the page number at the outside margin in the header, place the author's name (you) centered in the header of the even-numbered (left) pages, and place the book title centered in the header of the odd-numbered (right-hand) pages.

For non-fiction, I looked at several books that fall generally into the category of "history." I avoided books that were aimed at children, books that were advertised as being for advanced placement history classes, and several that looked like memoirs or family histories rather than general audience history books. What I found was that, as with the romance novels, only one put the page number in the footer. All the others put the page number in the header, at the outside margin. Beyond that, there was little consistency. About half put the author's name centered in the header of the left-hand pages and the book title centered in the header of the right-hand pages. The others put the book title centered in the header of the left-hand pages, and the chapter title centered in the header of the right-hand pages.

I favor putting the book title in the header of the even-numbered pages and chapter titles in the header of the odd-numbered pages. Personally, I also favor putting the page numbers in the footer, but incorporating the page number into the headers allows eliminating the footers, reducing the height of the bottom margin and resulting in a few more lines of print per page, which reduces the total page count.

Creating Headers

LibreOffice Writer handles headers and footers very differently from the way it's done in Microsoft Word. The differences are so profound that I think this topic deserves its own chapter. In fact, for a long time I was convinced that it was impossible in LibreOffice Writer to set up alternating headers for books. The impetus to write this book was my desire to save other authors the many hours I wasted trying to figure out how to handle headers correctly.

There are two ways headers are commonly placed in books. In LibreOffice Writer they are handled differently, so they will be discussed separately.

For fiction books, by far the most common approach is to put the author's name in one header (usually the left-hand pages) and the book title in the header of the opposite pages (usually the right-hand pages). This isn't exceptionally difficult in LibreOffice Writer.

Non-fiction books, however, often are a bit more complicated. It's commonplace with non-fiction books to put the book title as the header on left-hand pages and the title of the current chapter as the header on right-hand pages. This is simple in Microsoft Word; once you know how to do it in Writer it's not terribly difficult, but the procedure is incredibly arcane and counter-intuitive.

I'll explain how to do each separately.

Fiction

As explained in the chapter on Page Styles, headers (and footers) are activated for each page style from a tab in the "Page Styles" dialogue window. This tells Writer that a left-hand page or a right-hand page will display a header, but it does *not* tell Writer what text to display in the headers. Where the headers will be the same for every chapter, there are two ways to accomplish this:

Method Number 1:

The "brute force" method: Simply put the cursor in the header area of one of the pages, and type in the information you want to display (the author's name or the title of the book).

Method Number 2:

This method is a bit more complicated, but it relates to the way to handle changing headers for non-fiction books, so it's a good idea to learn it.

Before entering headers using this method, you must edit the document properties (the "metadata"). On the menu bar at the top of the screen, open the "File" tab, and click "Properties."

In the Properties dialogue window, fill in as many of the fields as you have information for. This information will be transferred later, when you convert the file to either PDF format for printing or to the EPUB format for digital publication. For the purpose of creating headers, the two fields that must be filled in at this time are "Title" (enter the exact title of the book) and "Contributor" (your name, as the author, exactly as you want it to appear on the outside cover and on the title page)

Click "OK."

Now you're ready to enter headers.

- Headers can only be entered on pages for which "Headers" has been activated through Page Styles. (If you can't click at the top of the page to enter a header, double check that the page style is set to a style that allows headers.)

- Click in the header area to place the mouse cursor where the header should be placed. You can use the alignment icons in the menu to locate the header at the left margin, in the center of the page, or at the right margin.
- On the menu bar at the top of the screen, click "Insert" and then hold the mouse cursor over "Field" (about three-quarters of the way down, toward the bottom).
- Click on "Title" for the header where the book title is supposed to appear. Click "First author" for the header where the author's name is supposed to appear. If the information was entered correctly in the file properties, the book title and author's name will now be displayed in the headers.

Non-Fiction

Displaying chapter titles in the headers of non-fiction books can't be done by just typing the chapter title into a header. What happens if you do that is that every chapter will display the same title. If you edit the chapter title in one chapter, that change will be displayed in the header of every chapter.

Instead, follow Method 2 from above, but with a minor change.

- Click in the header area to place the mouse cursor where the header should be placed. You can use the alignment icons in the menu to locate the header at the left margin, in the center of the page, or at the right margin.
- On the menu bar at the top of the screen, click "Insert" and then hold the mouse cursor over

"Field" (about three-quarters of the way down, toward the bottom).

- For the header where the book title should be displayed, click on "Title." If the information was entered correctly in the file properties, the book title and autor's name will now be displayed in the headers.
- On the menu bar at the top of the screen, click "Insert" and then hold the mouse cursor over "Field" again.
- For the headers where the chapter titles are supposed to be displayed, click on "More fields." This opens a second dialogue window.
- Select "Heading" in the left-hand column ('Type"), and select "Heading contents" in the right-hand column ("Format").
- In the field below the right-hand column, verify that "Up to level" is set to "1."
- Click "Insert" at the lower right corner of the window.

With this field entered, Writer will go through the document and enter whatever is typed into the chapter title in the header. This requires that chapter titles must use the "Heading 1" paragraph style, and that nothing else in each chapter uses the 'Heading 1 style."

7 — Typography (Fonts)

Once the page layout has been set up to your satisfaction, it's time to decide on what fonts you want to use for the main body text of the book, and for chapter headings. There are a lot of fonts available to any computer user, and the font you choose can make a big difference in whether your book is easy to read or hard on the eyes.

Fundamentals

It's best to use only two—or three, at most—fonts throughout a book. Using too many fonts can overwhelm the reader's eyes and senses. In designing the interior of a book, the goal of the designer is to not draw the reader's attention to the design, or to the fonts. The goal is to make the book as easy to read as possible. Some fonts are simply more readable than others, so choosing the right font is an important decision.

Book design professionals and graphic artists have determined that for reading large blocks of text (such as a book), "serif" typefaces are better that "sans serif" typefaces. Let's begin by understanding what those terms mean. A serif is a small transverse extension at the ends of the strokes forming each letter or character. "Sans" is the French word for "without," so a sans serif letter is a letter that does not have an embellishment at the ends of the strokes. For example, in the fonts that seem to have become the effective default choices for many computers and for many computer users,

Times New Roman is a serif typeface, and Arial is a sans-serif typeface.

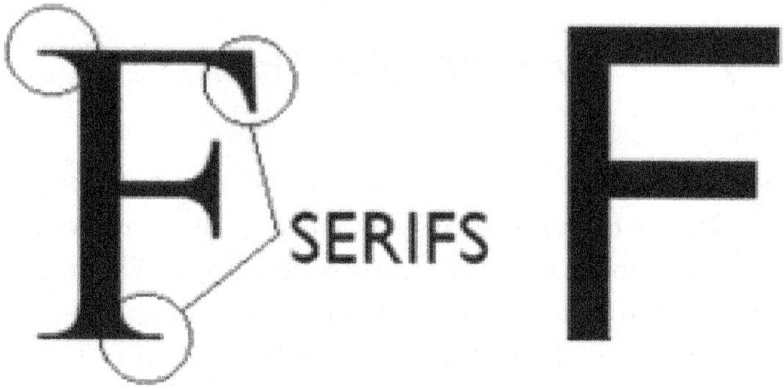

First, it helps to understand the terminology. The style of the letters—the design—is properly called the "typeface." In the early days of printing presses, each individual letters was carved or cast on a separate block of wood or metal. The job of the typesetter was, quite literally, to set all those individual chunks of wood or metal in rows to make up words and sentences. The term "font" referred to a specific combination of typeface, type size, and attributes (such as italics or bold face). This means that, for example, Times New Roman is a typeface; Times New Roman 12-point Regular, Times New Roman 14-point Regular, and Times New Roman 10-point Italic are three separate fonts, even though they are variations of the same basic typeface.

Today, thanks to digital type technology, the term "font" has become largely interchangeable with "typeface." In the old days, a printer had to buy a box of type just for Times New Roman 12-point Regular. If he also wanted Times New Roman 14-point Regular he had to buy another box of type. If he wanted Times New Roman 10-point Italic, he had to buy a third box of type. Today, computer users have a wide variety of typefaces available as standard with their operating system and, thanks to the magic of technology such as

TrueType and OpenType, a single font can be scaled from too small to read all the way to too large to fit on a standard sheet or paper. We are blessed—and spoiled. We have so many fonts available to us, in fact, that deciding which to use can be an almost paralyzing decision.

Typeface Selection

For many computers and word processing programs, it seems that Times New Roman has become the default font (or typeface). Aspiring self-publishers can just use Times New Roman but, in reality, although it will get the job done it isn't a good choice. The reason it isn't a good choice lies in the history of the typeface.

The name itself reflects the history. "Roman" is often used to refer to the standard, vertical variant of a typeface. In 1931, The Times newspaper of London adopted a new typeface that was designed specifically for their use. It was for The Times, it was new, and the basic variation was the Roman font, so it became known as "Times New Roman." Being intended for a newspaper, it was designed expressly to be legible in small type sizes and in the comparatively narrow columns found on the pages of newspaper. Consequently, although Times New Roman can be used to set an entire book, the letters are a bit narrower and the resulting text is a bit too compact for optimal reading when used to set an entire page.

I know two authors who have self-published novels set in Times New Roman, so it certainly can be done. That said, book design professionals generally recommend using other readily-available fonts to set the body text of books. Then the problem becomes deciding which font to use instead of good old Times New Roman.

The goal in font (typeface) selection is not to attract attention to the type, but simply to make the text easy to read. One professional summed it up this way:

> "Set running text in one of the hundreds of standard text faces (including humanistic sans serif designs), at a reasonable size — usually between 9- and 12-point. Leave the letter fit alone (don't use tracking), don't enter two spaces between words or sentences, and don't allow justification to enlarge word spaces unreasonably. Use a measure that allows for 60 to 70 characters per line and add a couple of points of leading. Indent paragraphs (all except the first after a heading, anyway) by one em or a pica, and allow for reasonable margins so readers have a place to hold the book. Avoid reader distractions like typewriter quotes and apostrophes or double hyphens where dashes ought to be.
>
> "All these factors work together. If you use a typeface that seems to be harder to read than average—Bodoni, for example—you can compensate by taking pains with spacing, adding leading, or making other adjustments. If you're pretty sure the work will need to be read by people with impaired vision, avoid low contrast and small sizes. If you anticipate poor lighting, avoid small type and designs with fine hairlines, and don't use colored inks or papers."

Part of establishing the interior design is the number of words and the number of characters per line. As usual, even published authorities don't always agree on what's best or ideal. There is a consensus that for single column book body text line length should be more than five words and less than fifteen words. The character count is a better criterion, and here is where there is less agreement among experts.

Some sources suggest a range of 40 to 75 characters per line. A more typical suggested range is 50 to 75 characters per line, and at least one source cites 65 characters per line as being ideal. This is where you have to balance the choice of typeface (font), type size, and margin widths to achieve an average character count per line that falls within the suggested optimum range. Kathleen Tinkel, quoted above, mentions a study that showed a range of 60 to 70 characters per line made reading easier. That's a good target range, but don't panic if you have a few lines that are 58 characters or a few that are 72 characters.

How do you know what the character count is? You can count each character (and space) in a line manually, but that's work. Word processing software can do the work for you. In LibreOffice Writer, the word count and the character count are both constantly displayed in a small window in the toolbar across the bottom of the LibreOffice window. When a section of text is selected (highlighted), this display changes to show the number of words and characters in just the selected text. These statistics can also be accessed from the menu bar at the top of the LibreOffice window, under Tools > Word Count. The pop-up window will display the total number of words and the number of characters in the entire document. However, if you select a section of text before you choose this function, it will also show statistics for the selected text only. To make it easy, select five or ten lines, get the number of characters, and then divide by five or ten to see the number of characters per line.

Especially for print, experimenting with different type faces (fonts) can change the character count per line. In the same type size, different fonts have different character widths and different character spacing. (This is referred to as the "font metrics.")

To save you searching through endless articles and directories of fonts, I have researched numerous articles and sifted the contents to come up with a list of five very readable fonts that seem to make everyone's list for novels and general reading—plus a couple of alternates. The preferred contenders are Baskerville Old Face, Caslon, Georgia, Book Antiqua, and Palatino Linotype.

Another classic typeface that I like very much is Goudy Old Style. Unfortunately, the version of this typeface on my computer does not include true italics. Computer technology can simulate italics by simply slanting the characters, but they don't look nearly as good as an italic font that's designed to harmonize with the corresponding Roman (upright) font. Avoid using any font that doesn't provide true italics.

For text that is likely to be read in poor lighting or by people with poor eyesight, and for textbooks, two other typefaces to consider are Century Schoolbook and Bookman Old Face. (This book is set in Century Schoolbook, 11-point, with 1.10 line spacing.)

Licenses

We don't tend to think about it, but fonts—or typefaces—are artwork. Each font is different, and each was designed by someone who went through much the same creative process that you went through in writing your book. This means that typefaces are intellectual property and, as such, they can be copyrighted. And most fonts are copyrighted. We are allowed to use fonts in typesetting our books only if we have a license from the owner of the font to use it for the purpose for which we intend to use it.

The most basic collections of fonts that we all have access to consist of whatever fonts came pre-loaded on our computers, usually included with the operating system. Windows includes a large number of fonts, MacOS includes a number of fonts. Linux and iOS include a number of fonts. Many of the fonts included with these operating systems are the same. The publishers of the respective operating systems generally have contracted with the owners of the copyrights to "bundle" the fonts with their operating systems. In turn, the publishers of the operating systems license registered users of the respective operating systems to use the fonts ... but only in accordance with the licensing agreement, which—of course—nobody ever reads. This is where it gets sticky.

We think of Microsoft Windows as just "Windows" but, in fact, under Windows 10 there are several different versions:

- Windows 10 Home
- Windows 10 Mobile (for cell phones and small tablets)
- Windows 10 Pro
- Windows 10 Enterprise
- Windows 10 Education
- Windows 10 Mobile Enterprise
- Windows 10 IoT Core

Most of these versions of Windows include the same fonts. However, the End User License Agreement (EULA) is different with respect to the use of the fonts. For versions of Windows intended for home, student, and personal use, the fonts can be used for any personal, non-commercial purpose but they may NOT be used for commercial purposes, nor can they be embedded in PDFs or EPUB files. Selling books is a commercial use; the fonts included with Windows technically can be used for commercial purposes only if your version of Windows is a business version (Windows 10 Pro or Windows 10 Enterprise).

Previous editions of Windows included different assortments of fonts. If you are using an older computer that has gone through updates and upgrades of Windows, it is entirely possible that you may have on your system fonts from an older version of Windows professional even though you are currently using Windows 10 Home.

To make it even more confusing, Microsoft Office also includes fonts, other than those that are included with Windows. And, like Windows, the fonts that come with Microsoft Office are allowed to be used for commercial purposes only if your version of Microsoft Office is a business version: Microsoft 365 Professional, Office Home and Business, or Office Professional. Microsoft 365 Personal and Office Home & Student are not licensed for commercial use.

As I discuss in the next section, not all font licenses are equal. For example, the license from one web site that provides free fonts is completely uninformative: "License: These fonts are neither public domain nor shareware. They may not be transferred to third parties. But we're always pleased when people tell friends and acquaintances about [website] and of course you're welcome to link to us." That tells us precisely nothing whatsoever about the actual terms of the license—so I sent them an e-mail and I asked. The response was the following: "PDF yes, e-book no, webfont no, printing yes, including commercial."

As a result, I had to decide not to use any free fonts from that site, because I can't legally use them to generate e-books. If I can't use a font to create an e-book or a web site—the font is useless to me. Don't download it, don't save it, don't even have it on your computer. Find an alternative.

Sources

In the real world, it's extremely unlikely that anyone seeing a book typeset in a font from Microsoft Windows or Microsoft Office will know or care if your version of the software is a home/personal version or a business version. But you should be aware of the distinction, because you may wish to explore fonts other than those already on your computer. There are numerous sites on the Internet from which you can download hundreds of fonts, entirely free. These include, but are not limited to:

- 1001 Fonts
- Font Squirrel
- Fontsov

You have to be careful when downloading fonts from these (and similar) sites, because not all fonts are created equal. These sites don't own the copyrights to the fonts they make available, and the licensing for the fonts isn't the same for all. Some fonts are licensed only for personal use, some are licensed for commercial use in print but not embedded into a e-book, and others may be licensed for all commercial purposes. To keep yourself completely in the clear legally, you should only download fonts that are licensed for all commercial purposes. On Font Squirrel, it appears that all the fonts they list are licensed for all commercial purposes, but it's wise to review the license for each font before downloading it. On Fontsov, you have to check a filter to limit the fonts you see to only those licensed for commercial use. On 1001 Fonts, there's a box toward the upper left on the screen that you have to check to see only fonts licensed for commercial use.

In my case, the computer I am using started out with Windows XP and Microsoft Office Professional 2003. I then upgraded the operating system to Windows 7 and then again to Windows 10, and I have upgraded Microsoft Office to 2010, 2013, 2016, and 2019. Through the upgrades, all the fonts that came with each version have stayed on the computer. The result is that I have a tremendous number of fonts, and I have no idea which of them are licensed for commercial use and which are only for personal use.

When I began self-publishing my writing, I knew that I wanted to feel comfortable that I wasn't infringing on a font designer's copyright by using a font in one of my books that isn't licensed to me for commercial purposes. My solution was to purchase a collection of professional fonts (7,500 of them, in fact) that are all licensed for any and all commercial purposes. This collection was priced at what I considered a very reasonable price (currently $34.95), considering the peace of mind it gives me over the prospect of unwittingly committing font piracy. The collection is named MegaFont NOW and it comes from the German company, SoftMaker (the same company that produces the FreeOffice office suite).

Of course, it isn't necessary to purchase 7,500 fonts to typeset one or even ten books. A tremendous number of those 7,500 fonts are fonts that I will almost certainly never, ever consider using for anything I'm likely to design. For the fonts that I will use, though, I consider it to be money well spent—especially considering that some of the fonts in the collection include outline versions and true small caps.

I'm sure there are other font collections available (in fact, over the years I have previously purchased several). I mention MegaFont NOW as an example of an affordable way to completely avoid questions about the license of the font or fonts you want to use in your book. But that can come later in your career as a writer. For just getting started, you should already have at least a couple or three of the commonly-suggested book fonts already on your computer, so go ahead and use one.

Type Size

An important decision that has to be made is the size of the type used for the body of the book. Kathleen Tinker's article (quoted above) suggests a type size range of 9- to 12-points for body text. Elsewhere in the same article she commented that even 12-point type is large enough that it's on the borderline of becoming difficult to read. On the other hand, the laws of some states stipulate 10-point type as the smallest size allowed for consumer contracts because anything smaller is too difficult for many people to read. I suggest that the range for type size in the body text of most books should be 9.5-point to 11.5-point—and I prefer to stay within the range from 10-point to 11-point.

The selection I quoted (above) from the late Kathleen Tinkel suggests formatting text so that the average line is between 60 and 70 characters (and 65 is often cited as being optimum). Word processing programs generally show type sizes in whole numbers in the drop-down menu for selecting type size. That can be overridden. TrueType and OpenType fonts allow them to be increased and decreased in increments of one-half point, so if 10 point is too small but 11 point is too large ... just highlight the font size in the style menu and type in "10.5."

What's "right" for your book will be a subjective decision. Some experimentation is needed, because fonts don't all display the same. I recently printed out a sample of two similar fonts; to make them display the same number of characters per line and to appear to be the same size, I had to set one of them in 14-point type and the other in 15-point type.

Select the typeface you want to use, format your body text in that typeface, and then experiment with changing the type size and the line spacing (see below) until the result looks right to you. If possible, print out a couple of sample pages illustrating different combinations and ask friends or relatives which combination looks best to them.

Line Spacing/Leading

Most word processing programs default to setting the type with the lines single-spaced (unless you have changed the settings in the default template). Depending on the typeface selected, standard single-spaced lines may be a little too close together for easiest reading. Articles on typography discuss adding "leading" to increase the vertical distance between lines. However, most word processing software doesn't use the term "leading," but they do allow customizing the space between lines. In LibreOffice Writer, this is set in the Paragraph Style dialogue box. I suggest starting with a setting of 1.1 or 1.15—if that's too loose or too tight, adjust up or down in increments of .02 or .05.

An easy test is to save a few pages of your manuscript as a separate file, format that file to the page size, layout, font and font size you are considering, and print two pages. Cut the two pages to the trim size you have chosen, staple them together right at the inside edge of the paper, and then look at it as if you are reading your book. You can do this for multiple options, to experiment with your choices of margins, typeface, font size, and line spacing.

Hyphenation

When text is left-justified, the spaces between words are consistent and each line of text ends where the last full word falls. This is what leads to the ragged, uneven right margins that we call "ragged right." When the style is changed so that body text is fully justified, the word processing software adjusts the spacing between words to bring the last word of each line out to the right-hand margin. Especially in lines that include long words, the result can be that the spaces between the words become too large to look right.

The solution is to use hyphens to break the last word in certain lines so the spaces between the words in the line look more proportionate to the text. All major word processing programs have a way of turning on automatic hyphenation. It should be turned on for any documents that will be formatted as fully-justified, and especially for books that will be set fully-justified.

In LibreOffice Writer, hyphenation is found on the "Text Flow" tab, in the "Paragraph Style" dialogue window.

Common Mistakes

The good thing about modern computers, word processing software, and desktop publishing software is that they offer everyone instant access to dozens of professionally-designed fonts. If the fonts that came pre-installed on your computer aren't enough, there are literally thousands of other fonts that can be downloaded for free from the internet.

The bad thing about modern computers, word processing software, and desktop publishing software is that they offer everyone instant access to dozens of professionally-designed fonts. If the fonts that came pre-installed on your computer aren't enough, there are literally thousands of other fonts that can be downloaded for free from the internet.

There is a natural tendency to want to experiment with unusual fonts, and to set different parts of a document in different typefaces. This is usually not a good idea. Years ago I read an article on designing advertising in which the author referred to what he called the "slick but bad presentation." What he was talking about was creating a page, or a single panel on a page, in which the designer used a half dozen or more fonts. The result is something that's too "busy" and jumbled for easy comprehension. Remember, the reason we put words on paper or on a computer screen is to convey information. As the typesetter or page designer, our job is to make the words as easy to read and understand as possible. Throwing too many fonts at the reader just confuses the eye and interferes with reading comprehension.

As I wrote at the start of this chapter, it's best to use only two—or possibly three, at most—fonts throughout a book.

~ ~ ~ ~ ~

Don't use fonts from Google for printed books. You *can*, but there are better choices.

Google Fonts offers fonts that are completely free, BUT ... they aren't optimized for print. Google Fonts are optimized for display on a computer screen, tablet, or e-book reader. Can you use them to generate a printed book? Yes, it is possible. However, the quality of the printed results won't be as good as the quality of fonts that were created primarily for printing.

~ ~ ~ ~ ~

Choose typefaces that offer a complete set of fonts.

The two major types of fonts used on computers today are TrueType fonts and OpenType fonts. If you have fonts installed on your computer, they are almost certainly one of these two types. One of the attributes of both TrueType fonts and OpenType fonts is that when the font doesn't offer an actual, designed subset for bold, italic, or bold-italic, the computer can manipulate the font to generate an approximation of any of the above. The quality, however, is not very good. These computer-generated approximations may be tolerable when used in a letter or even an informal report, but they are basically ugly and they are immediately obvious to any viewer who knows anything at all about either typography or computers.

Try to use only fonts that offer at least four separate files to comprise the font set: a Regular (the standard, upright font that will be used for 90 percent or more of the text), an Italic, a Bold, and a Bold Italic. To see what variations are included with a font, on Windows computers simply open a file explorer application (such as Windows Explorer) and navigate to C:\Windows\Fonts. This will display a list of all the fonts installed on your computer. The second column, "Font Style," shows what variations are included.

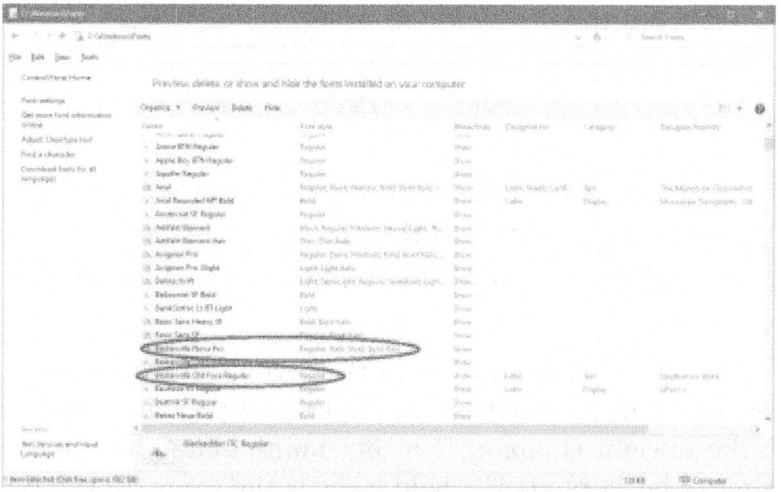

Baskerville is a classic typeface that's still a good choice for books. The above image is a screen shot of the font listing on my computer. Notice that the font "Baskerville Old Style" shows that the font family only includes a Regular version. If I were to use this font in a book, anywhere I used italics or boldface type, they would be computer-generated by manipulating the standard "Regular" (Roman, upright) font.

But I have another Baskerville font, Baskerville Nova Pro, which came as part of a collection of "professional" fonts I purchased some time ago. "Baskerville Nova Pro" includes Regular, Italic, Bold, and Bold Italic versions of the font. I have published several books using Baskerville Nova Pro in 11.5-point, with the line spacing set to 1.1.

Here's the difference:

> Lorem ipsum *dolor sit amet,* consectetur adipiscing elit, **sed do** eiusmod tempor incididunt ut ***labore et dolore*** magna aliqua

> Lorem ipsum *dolor sit amet,* consectetur adipiscing elit, **sed do** eiusmod tempor incididunt ut ***labore et dolore*** magna aliqua.

The upper passage is set in Baskerville Old Face. Notice how in the italics the vertical strokes are the same shape as in the upright (Roman) font, but manipulated by the computer to be slanted. The bold italic is the same. In the Baskerville Nova Pro type, the italic characters have been specifically designed with rounded serifs and followers to look better as italics.

Computers can also generate "small caps" from standard fonts. These don't look too bad, but a typography professional can usually spot them instantly. Some true "professional" font sets include Small Caps in addition to true Italics, Boldface, and Bolt Italics. Although a professional book designer would never use computer-generated small caps in a commercial book, they get the job done and, in my opinion, they are good enough for at least ninety percent of authors who are self-publishing through the print-on-demand channels. One word of caution about computer-generated small caps, however, is that they may not convert correctly into the EPUB format when exporting the e-book manuscript into the final EPUB version.

I think they are perfectly acceptable for self-published, print-on-demand books, but if you will also publish the same book as an e-book (either Kindle or EPUB), it would be wise to save a separate copy of the manuscript file and eliminate any small caps that were computer-generated.

8 — Finishing Touches

There are a couple of added enhancements that can help to transform your print-on-demand book from something that looks slapped together into something that looks like a "real" book. They aren't difficult to accomplish, and they can help your book stand out from the quick and dirty books churned out by other self-published authors.

Drop Caps

"Drop caps" is short for "dropped capitals," referring to the practice of capitalizing the first letter of a new chapter. In its simplest form, a drop cap uses the same font as the book's body text and simply enlarges it, but there are additional ways to dress up drop caps.

The basic creation of drop caps is built into most word processing programs. In LibreOffice Writer, drop caps are found by clicking on the "Drop Caps" tab of the Paragraph Styles dialogue window.

Two examples of drop caps are shown on the following page. Many variations can be achieved if you are willing to experiment, but it isn't necessary to go overboard. A simple two- or three-line drop cap such as in the first example adds a professional touch to any book and is easy to accomplish.

2

Lorem ipsum dolor sit amet, consectetur adipiscing elit, sed do eiusmod tempor incididunt ut labore et dolore magna aliqua. Posuere lorem ipsum dolor sit amet consectetur adipiscing elit. Eget est lorem ipsum dolor sit amet consectetur. Auctor elit sed vulputate mi sit amet. Leo a diam sollicitudin tempor id. Sodales neque sodales ut etiam sit. Sit amet nisl purus in. Commodo odio aenean sed adipiscing diam donec adipiscing. Non blandit massa enim nec dui nunc mattis. Id nibh tortor id aliquet lectus.

Ipsum suspendisse ultrices gravida dictum fusce ut placerat orci nulla. Facilisis sed odio morbi quis commodo odio. Amet consectetur adipiscing elit

2

Lorem ipsum dolor sit amet, consectetur adipiscing elit, sed do eiusmod tempor incididunt ut labore et dolore magna aliqua. Posuere lorem ipsum dolor sit amet consectetur adipiscing elit. Eget est lorem ipsum dolor sit amet consectetur. Auctor elit sed vulputate mi sit amet. Leo a diam sollicitudin tempor id. Sodales neque sodales ut etiam sit. Sit amet nisl purus in. Commodo odio aenean sed adipiscing diam donec adipiscing. Non blandit massa enim nec dui nunc mattis. Id nibh tortor id aliquet lectus.

Ipsum suspendisse ultrices gravida dictum fusce ut placerat orci nulla. Facilisis sed odio morbi quis commodo odio. Amet consectetur adipiscing elit

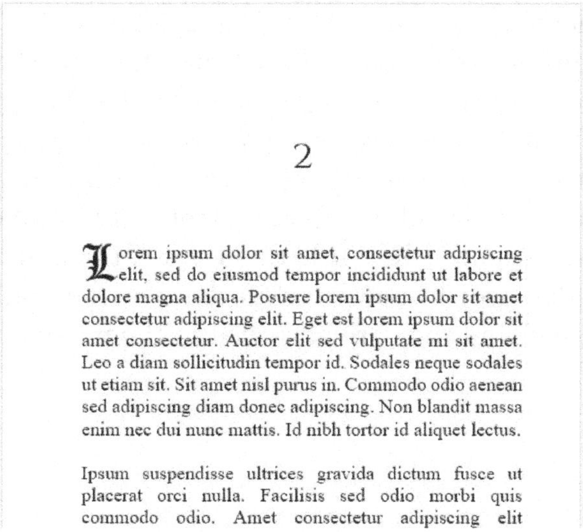
2

Lorem ipsum dolor sit amet, consectetur adipiscing elit, sed do eiusmod tempor incididunt ut labore et dolore magna aliqua. Posuere lorem ipsum dolor sit amet consectetur adipiscing elit. Eget est lorem ipsum dolor sit amet consectetur. Auctor elit sed vulputate mi sit amet. Leo a diam sollicitudin tempor id. Sodales neque sodales ut etiam sit. Sit amet nisl purus in. Commodo odio aenean sed adipiscing diam donec adipiscing. Non blandit massa enim nec dui nunc mattis. Id nibh tortor id aliquet lectus.

Ipsum suspendisse ultrices gravida dictum fusce ut placerat orci nulla. Facilisis sed odio morbi quis commodo odio. Amet consectetur adipiscing elit

All in all, drop caps offer a number of ways to dress up the appearance of your book with nothing more than a few clicks of the mouse.

Small Caps

Just as “Drop Caps” is an abbreviation for “Dropped Capitals,” so “Small Caps” is an abbreviation for “Small Capitals.” Using small capital letters for the text of the first few words in the first sentence of a new chapter (either alone or in combination with a drop cap) is another way to subtly enhance the typesetting of your book at help convey to the reader that your book wasn’t published by a novice.

In professional typesetting, small caps are separate fonts, consisting of all capital characters but approximately two-thirds the height of the standard capital letters in the font. In a true small caps font, the small caps are designed so the stroke widths of the letters are the same as the stroke widths of the full-size characters. Unfortunately, none of the fonts that come standard with Windows or Microsoft

Office include true small caps. The good news for self-published authors is that the TrueType and OpenType fonts that come with the operating system can be manipulated to simulate small caps. Professional book designers complain that, because these small caps are scaled down in all respects from their full-size equivalents, the stroke widths aren't the same width. While this is true, the reality is that most readers won't know the difference — especially if your story is good and they are absorbed in the narrative.

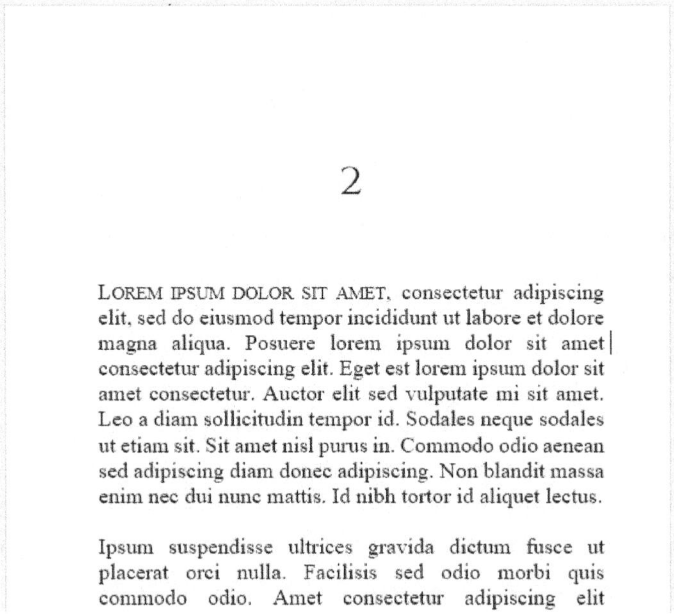

2

LOREM IPSUM DOLOR SIT AMET, consectetur adipiscing elit, sed do eiusmod tempor incididunt ut labore et dolore magna aliqua. Posuere lorem ipsum dolor sit amet consectetur adipiscing elit. Eget est lorem ipsum dolor sit amet consectetur. Auctor elit sed vulputate mi sit amet. Leo a diam sollicitudin tempor id. Sodales neque sodales ut etiam sit. Sit amet nisl purus in. Commodo odio aenean sed adipiscing diam donec adipiscing. Non blandit massa enim nec dui nunc mattis. Id nibh tortor id aliquet lectus.

Ipsum suspendisse ultrices gravida dictum fusce ut placerat orci nulla. Facilisis sed odio morbi quis commodo odio. Amet consectetur adipiscing elit

And, of course, small caps can be combined with drop caps:

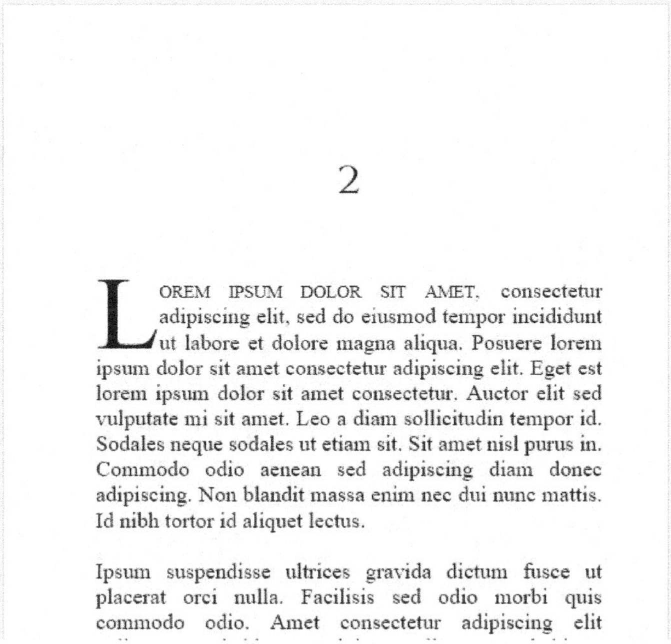

2

LOREM IPSUM DOLOR SIT AMET, consectetur adipiscing elit, sed do eiusmod tempor incididunt ut labore et dolore magna aliqua. Posuere lorem ipsum dolor sit amet consectetur adipiscing elit. Eget est lorem ipsum dolor sit amet consectetur. Auctor elit sed vulputate mi sit amet. Leo a diam sollicitudin tempor id. Sodales neque sodales ut etiam sit. Sit amet nisl purus in. Commodo odio aenean sed adipiscing diam donec adipiscing. Non blandit massa enim nec dui nunc mattis. Id nibh tortor id aliquet lectus.

Ipsum suspendisse ultrices gravida dictum fusce ut placerat orci nulla. Facilisis sed odio morbi quis commodo odio. Amet consectetur adipiscing elit

Ligatures

In traditional typesetting, certain combinations of letters tend to run together and type designers back in the days of hand-carved type sometimes designed special blocks that made those combinations a bit fancier. On computers, some TrueType and OpenType fonts include additional glyphs for ligatures. To make your book look just a bit more professional, you may decide to take the time to convert your book to use ligatures if the font you have chosen offers them.

The following illustrates some of the ligatures available in the Times New Roman font:

Aesthetic	Æsthetic
Orthopaedic	Orthopædic
fine	ﬁne
flow	ﬂow
difficult	diﬃcult
affluent	aﬄuent

In this sample, the plain text words are on the left, and the same words with ligatures are in the right-hand column. Using ligatures is completely unnecessary, but those who are willing to expend the time and the effort to use them will have a book that carries another hallmark of having been designed by someone who knows what they're doing.

Unfortunately, putting ligatures into your text is a manual process, and it's tedious. It requires first identifying each ligature you want to use and manually inserting it to a blank line somewhere near the start of the document. This is done from the "Insert" tab on the ribbon, and choosing "Symbol" from the "Text" panel at the right-hand end of the ribbon. The default view will probably be some standard symbols such as the "at" symbol [@], the glyph for "section" [§], the copyright symbol [©], and a few more. Click on

"More" at the bottom to open up the font character map. Be sure the font box at the top shows the font you are using, then scroll through the map to find and select the characters you want. Once you have them available, you can individually copy each one and then use the search and replace function to go through the document and replace each letter combination with the corresponding ligature. Once all the ligatures have been placed, go back and delete the source line that contains just the ligature symbols.

Yes, it's work. Is it worth the time and the effort? For most people and for most books, probably not. For someone who really cares about making their book look as professional as possible, and who can afford to take the time to do it—it's a nice, subtle touch to set your work apart for everyone else.

~ ~ ~ ~ ~

As with most enhancements, if you overdo them they just look busy or fussy. Don't overdo. Used with restraint, drop caps and small caps can make a huge difference in making your book look like a professional product rather than the slap-dash effort of an amateur.

9 — Front Matter

As authors, we expend copious amounts of time and effort on creating, editing, and perfecting the text that comprises the body of our books. When a book is published, however, before the reader ever gets to the book itself there is a bunch of miscellaneous information that comes before the actual text of the book. Since this assemblage of miscellany is located at the front of the book, it is cleverly referred to as the "front matter." There are lists of what items go into the front matter and, naturally, not all authorities agree on the order in which they are presented. Also, depending on the type of book and the author's wishes and intentions, some front matter items are optional and may not be used at all.

What goes into the front matter?

- The title page (mandatory)
- The copyright page (mandatory)
- The dedication page (optional, but customary)
- Table of Contents (usually only in non-fiction books)
- An epigraph (optional)
- A preface (optional but customary)
- A foreword (optional)

Especially for print books, to the above list may be added

- A half title page (optional)
- A frontispiece (optional)
- An acknowledgements page
- A list of tables (non-fiction, optional)

- A list of illustrations (non-fiction, optional)
- An introduction
- Another half title page

What are these, and how should they be arranged? The following pages will explain what they are. The order in which I will discuss them is the order suggested by one of the sources I reviewed for what order the front matter should follow. As I commented above, not all sources agree on either the order of the items to be included. To facilitate my research, I entered into a spreadsheet the various items in the suggested order as cited in seven different web sites discussing publishing. One list, from TheBook-Designer.com, is more extensive than any of the others, so I am going to follow the order in which that site organized and discussed them.

Note that in print, the pages comprising the front matter are numbered using lower case Roman numerals rather than Arabic numbers. Pages such as the title page and copyright page are not numbered; the first numbered page should be the first page after the copyright page, whether that's a dedication page, an epigraph, a table of contents, or any other page that comprises the front matter.

Half Title Page

The title and the author's name both appear, of course, on the cover (or on the jacket, in the case of many hardcover books). In mass market paperbacks and many low-end and self-published paperback books, the first printed page is often the title page. In higher quality books, however, to sort of set the stage for the interior title page the book designer may make the first right-hand page a half title page. (Or the first right-hand page may simply be left blank.)

A half title page simply repeats the book's title, but not the author's name or any other information), usually using the same font or fonts as the title page but reduced in size/scale to two-thirds or one-half size. Its purpose is to provide a transition into the book.

I would not use a half title page for an e-book version.

The Frontispiece

A frontispiece is a page containing an illustration that sets the tone for a book and is almost always placed (if used) on the first left-hand page, facing the title page. This means that if your book layout doesn't include either a first half title page or a blank first page, there will not be a left-hand page facing the title page and you can't use a frontispiece illustration.

The use of a frontispiece is always optional. There is especially no reason for it in an e-book.

The Title Page

While a half title page is optional, the actual title page is not optional. The title page includes the full title of the book, the author's name, and may also include the name (and possibly the logo) of the publisher. The layout and type style of the title page usually mirrors that of the outer cover, but title pages usually don't include the artwork (if the cover includes artwork). Unlike a half title page, on the title page the book title is not reduced in size or scale; both the title and the author's name should appear at approximately the same size and layout as on the outer cover.

The Copyright Page

Especially if you have copyrighted your book, the copyright page is not optional. This is the page on which the author (or other copyright owner, if applicable) states the copyright and the year in which the copyright was created. The copyright page is always the left-hand page immediately following the title page.

The copyright page is also where the publication information is placed. This includes the Library of Congress Control Number (LCCN), if you obtained one, the ISBN number, any legal disclaimers (such as, for example, something like, "This is a work of fiction. Any resemblance between the characters in this book and real persons, living or dead, is accidental and coincidental.") The copyright page should also include the publisher's full name, physical address, and (if applicable) mailing address. You may want to also include a web site address.

It is important to understand that any disclaimer you place on the copyright page is a legal statement. You put it there for the purpose of avoiding legal liability, such as for inadvertently libeling someone. If you can possibly afford it, it would be wise to have an attorney either draft or, at least, review the language of your disclaimer. If you can't afford to use an attorney, take the time to review and copy the disclaimers of as many books in your genre as possible. Write down the exact language, or take photos for reference. Look at the disclaimers in books from larger publishing houses rather than from indie self-publishers. The big publishing houses will have had their disclaimers drafted by corporate lawyers, so those will be the best examples on which to base your disclaimer.

The Dedication

Not every book has a dedication. If you choose to dedicate your book to someone, all that's needed is a simple paragraph, or even just one sentence. The dedication goes on the right-hand page facing the copyright page; a dedication usually comes before an epigraph, or a table of contents.

The Epigraph

An epigraph, if used, is a quotation that sets the tone for the book. An epigraph is optional. Some authors may choose to omit an epigraph in the front matter and, instead, place a brief epigraph at the beginning of each chapter. The choice is yours.

If I use an epigraph, I prefer to put it on the next right-hand page following the dedication. Many book designers, though, place the epigraph on the left-hand page facing either the table of contents, or the first page of the book body.

The Table of Contents

A table of contents is optional, for both print and digital formats. That said, my view is that it's never a bad idea to include a hyperlink table of contents for fiction, to allow readers to jump immediately to a specific chapter. For fiction in print, I don't think a table of contents is at all necessary. Where a table of contents is called for is in non-fiction and technical books, in which a reader might want to be able to open directly to a specific topic.

All the major word processing programs include the ability to automatically generate a table of contents, based on they styles used for the chapter headings and subheads. This is another very good reason to learn to use text styles to define your text rather than always leaving the style set to "Normal" or "Default" and then applying the style characteristics manually. Depending on the structure of your book, a table of contents may list only chapters, or it may be broken down into chapters and then sections within chapters.

The List of Figures

In publishing, "figures" refers to illustrations. These may be photographs, drawings, sketches, maps—any sort of graphic image. They may or may not include captions. If a book includes a large number of illustrations, it can be helpful to include a list of figures following the table of contents. If you do so, the list should include the figure number, a descriptive title (if the caption is too long), and for print books it should include the page number.

The List of Tables

Most books won't include many tables, so this won't be necessary. If your book does happen to include a large number of tables, it may be helpful to readers to include a list of tables that's separate from the table of contents and the list if figures. If you include a list of tables, it should be set up the same as the list of figures.

The Foreword

A foreword is a short essay written about the book by someone other than the author. A foreword is optional, and is perhaps more commonly used for non-fiction books rather than for fiction. If used, a foreword should be brief—typically one page, and not more than two pages. If used, a foreword should end with the name of the person who wrote it, the date, and the place of residence of the person who wrote the foreword.

As a rule, a foreword should be written by a recognized authority in the field covered by the book, and it should explain why the contents of the book will be of value to the reader in expanding their understanding of the topic or the field. Because the time of recognized experts in any technical field is valuable, unless you are an expert who has other experts as close, personal friends, it is customary for writers of forewords to be paid. The amount of the payment is a function of the fame and reputation of the author of the foreword, your own reputation in the field, the length of the foreword, and the value the foreword is likely to add to the book. A typical range might be between $100 and $500; do not blithely reach out to the world's foremost expert in your topic and expect that he or she will be overjoyed to write a foreword for you—an unknown in the field—out of the goodness of their heart.

The Preface

A preface is similar to a foreword, except that a preface is written by the author of the book. Like the foreword, a preface is optional. A preface is typically found in non-fiction books rather than in novels.

Authors may use a preface to explain how the book came into being: where they got the idea to write it, the reasons for writing it, the author's qualifications in the subject matter of the book, and perhaps a brief discussion of any research methodologies employed in compiling the material that comprises the book. Also like a foreword, a preface should be brief—one or two pages, at most.

If you include a preface, use it to tell readers why they should read your book. Use the preface to share your excitement about the subject matter, and let them know what they'll gain by reading your book.

Acknowledgements

Most authors consult with someone during the course of writing a book, either for research into matters the author doesn't fully understand, or editors and "beta" readers who helped review and polish the manuscript into its final form. The acknowledgements section is where the author lets readers know who helped him/her, and how, and where the author expresses thanks to those people.

The Introduction

An introduction is usually used in non-fiction books. The introduction can be used to inform the reader about how the book is organized, and what are the purposes and goals of the book. In teaching, instructors are advised to begin a class by explaining to the students what they are going to learn, then go on to teach the material, and then to end the class by reminding the students what they have just learned. The introduction to a book serves the same purpose as the first of the three parts of teaching: use the introduction to "tee up" the material, to prepare your readers for the more detailed information that will follow in the individual chapters.

How is the introduction different from the preface? The preface should be about you, the author, and the process of creating the book. The introduction is about the subject matter of the book. It's essentially a chapter before the first chapter, which is why it is part of the front matter rather than part of the book body.

The Prologue

Whereas an introduction is usually found in non-fiction books, fiction books often include a prologue to set the stage for the events that will take place in the body of the book. A prologue is the author's opportunity to relate the back story that's not part of the events in the book but which led up to the point in time where and when the book begins. In some cases, the prologue may also be a place to introduce one or two of the main characters—or it may be set far enough in the past that it introduces instead the ancestors of the book's main characters.

Authorities don't agree on whether a prologue belongs with the front matter, or with the book body. The only functional difference is whether a prologue (if you use one) is placed before or after the second half title page, and whether it gets numbered using lower case Roman numerals or Arabic numbers.

The Second Half Title Page

If you used a half title page just inside the front cover, then you might also want to use a second half title page to separate the front matter from the body of the book. If used, the second half title page should be an exact duplicate of the first half title page. The second half title page should not have a header, footer, or page number; it should only include the title of the book.

10 — Preparing For Publication

When submitting the finished manuscript to an on-line publishing service, it is important to submit the file in a format the publisher will accept. The file requirements for printed books are generally different from the requirements for e-books, and not all e-books use the same format. Before uploading your manuscript, be sure that your manuscript file is in the correct format, and that you have checked it for errors.

Amazon KDP can accept manuscript files in the following formats for the interior of printed books: PDF, RTF, DOCX, TXT, EPUB, and HTML. Cover files for printed books must be in PDF format, or you can use KDP's on-line Cover Creator to generate your cover

Barnes and Noble Press has time constraints on uploads. Manuscript and cover files for printed books must be uploaded at least ten days before the scheduled date of publication. For the interior of printed books, Barnes and Noble Press will accept files in the DOCX, TXT, RTF, HTML and PDF formats. Cover files for printed books must be in PDF format; JPG and other graphics file formats are not accepted.

Draft2Digital (D2D) accepts the following files types for book interiors: .DOC, .DOCX, .RTF, .OTF, and TXT for either print or e-book. D2D also accepts files in the .PDF format for printed books. According to the D2D web site, the .DOCX format is the most popular.

Table of Contents

For printed books, a table of contents is not usually needed or provided for novels. Tables of contents (as well as indexes) are more commonly found in non-fiction, technical and reference books. For a non-fiction technical or reference book that calls for a table of contents in the print version, the table of contents will not be hyperlinked but will include page number references for each chapter and section listed in the table of contents. The major word processing programs all include a function for generating a table of contents based on the use of paragraph styles to define chapter and section headings. I very much recommend using this automated table of contents generation function rather than trying to laboriously go through a long manuscript to find each chapter and subhead, copy the title to the table of contents, and then manually enter the page number.

To avoid having to repeat the process after making editorial changes, I suggest saving the table of contents step for the end. Don't generate the table of contents until the manuscript has been completed and edited, and (for printed books) after the book interior has been completely formatted to the desired trim size, typeface, and font size. Otherwise, the page numbers will be incorrect.

Creating a Table of Contents

LibreOffice Writer can generate a table of contents automatically. The best way to generate a table of contents is to apply the predefined heading paragraph styles, such as "Heading 1", to the paragraphs that you want to include in your table of contents. After you apply these styles, you can then create a table of contents.

To Insert a Table of Contents

- Click in your document where you want to create the table of contents.
- Choose Insert > Table of Contents and Index > Table of Contents, Index or Bibliography, and then click the Type tab.
- Select "Table of Contents" in the Type box.
- Select any options that you want.
- Click OK.

If you want to use a different paragraph style as a table of contents entry, select the Additional Styles check box in the Create from area, and then click the Assign styles button next to the check box. In the Assign Styles dialog, click the style in the Style list, and then click the index level for the selected style.

LibreOffice creates the table of contents entries based on the outline level of the paragraph style and the paragraph contents. If the paragraph is empty, it will not be included in the table of contents. To force the empty paragraph to be listed in the table of contents, manually add a space or a non-breaking space to the paragraph. Spaces added in the After text box of the Numbering tab in the Heading Numbering dialog will not work for this purpose, since they are part of the paragraph numbering, not the paragraph contents.

As soon as you confirm with "OK," the table of contents is inserted into the text. If a table of contents already exists, it will be updated at the existing position. For example:

The Love Life of Trees 1
In Spring.. 1
March 1
April 3
May 4
In Summer...................................... 7
In Autumn 10

Excerpt from a table of contents

Writer displays the headings on the left. To the right of each heading, the corresponding page number is displayed.

Converting the File for Upload

For printed books, although most of the print-on-demand services accept files in the Microsoft Word .DOCX format, they also all accept files in the .PDF format. I prefer to upload PDFs, because that gives me an opportunity to see what the final book is going to look like before I even upload the file and submit it to the service's quality check. LibreOffice Writer includes a function to export to PDF.

When converting the book interior to PDF for upload, especially if you have used fonts that were not included with your computer's operating system, be sure to learn how to embed the fonts in the PDF file. This is important because, even with a PDF file, if the fonts in the document aren't installed on the computer on which the file is being read, the system will substitute another font that it (the computer) thinks is the best near-equivalent. The substitute font is almost never going to be a true equivalent, so substitute fonts will wreak havoc on the formatting of your book. Amazon KDP requires that fonts be embedded in the file you upload for print.

In LibreOffice Writer, the Export to PDF menu choice opens a dialogue box with multiple options. There is no option that directly offers to embed fonts, but there is an option for PDF/A. The "A" stands for "Archival," and documents exported to PDF/A have fonts embedded.

Writer's export dialogue offers a choice of two non-PDF/A formats and four PDF/A formats. The best choice for uploading books for print seems to be the PDF/A-2b option.

- Go to File > Export As PDF
- Click the "General" tab

- In the "Range" section, be sure "All" is selected to ensure printing all pages
- In the "Images" section, leave all settings at the default
- "Watermark": Leave this field unchecked
- In the "General" section, select PDF/A-2b
- In the "Forms" section, do *not* check the box for "Create PDF form"
- "Structure": Check the boxes for "Export outlines" and for "Export automatically inserted blank pages"
- Click "Export" to create and save the PDF

11 — A Word About ISBNs

ISBN is the acronym for International Standard Book Number. An ISBN is to books much like a VIN (Vehicle Identification Number) is to an automobile. It isn't a legal requirement for a book to have an ISBN, but in practical terms a book can't be sold without one, because the ISBN is how booksellers find, order, and stock books and it is also how most libraries catalog books. Unless you are writing a book for the sole purpose of having a few copies printed to give away to family and friends ... you need an ISBN.

Each unique version of a book needs its own ISBN. This means that if you publish the same book in hardcover, trade (quality) paperback, and "mass market" paperback formats, you will need three ISBNs. E-books (Amazon Kindle, Barnes & Noble Nook, Kobo, Apple Books and others) do not require an ISBN. However, although other sources disagree, the director of my local public library as told me that most libraries acquire and catalog e-books by ISBN, so his recommendation is to assign a unique ISBN to digital editions, as well. Since a unique ISBN is required for each unique format of a title, this would mean one ISBN for a Kindle edition and a separate ISBN for an EPUB edition.

ISBNs are not distributed by the government, at least in the United States. In the United States, ISBN numbers are purchased through the ISBN provider R. R. Bowker, LLC. In the U.S., ISBNs have a cost, and it's not cheap. In fact, for self-publishing on a budget, purchasing the ISBN may be the single most expensive item in the process. Bowker charges $125 for a single ISBN. The unit price drops considerably if you purchase multiple ISBNs; Bowker currently offers ten ISBNs for $295, and blocks of 100 ISBNs for $575. Bowker also maintains the catalog of books in print, so an advantage to buying your own ISBNs from Bowker is that you can ensure that your book is listed in the industry-standard catalog as being in print and available — and that you are listed as the publisher.

In the United Kingdom and the Republic of Ireland, Nielsen Book Services Ltd is the ISBN distributor. Just to be different, Canada has one source for books in English and a separate provider in Quebec for books in French: Library and Archives Canada, and Bibiolthèque et Archives Nationales du Québec. Both can be accessed through a common Internet portal. In the U.K. and Ireland, Nielsen operates much like Bowker in the U.S.; a single ISBN costs £89.00, a block of ten costs £164.00, and a block of 100 costs £369.00. ISBNs for self-publishers who are permanent residents of Canada are free.

Whether or not to buy a single ISBN or a block of ISBNs depends on personal preferences. Both Amazon and Barnes & Noble ask authors if they have an ISBN for their book at the time the book is uploaded. If not, Amazon and Barnes & Noble will provide an ISBN — at no cost to the author. One problem with this is that the entity that owns the ISBN is officially the publisher so if you allow Amazon KDP to provide the ISBN for your print-on-demand book, Amazon KDP will forever be listed as the publisher. You will still own the copyright and you will still be listed as the author, but you will NOT be the publisher.

A second problem is confusion. If you publish the exact same book through Amazon KDP and through Barnes & Noble Press, each will assign an ISBN to the book in their system. Now you will have two ISBNs and two publishers associated with the same book. In my opinion, while accepting a free ISBN is obviously the cheapest way to get published (unless you are in Canada), it makes sense only if you never plan to offer the book through more than one service — or if you don't care about sales, and you just want to be able to have some books printed to give away.

The question of whether or not to assign ISBNs to digital books is even murkier. Despite what my library director told me, the vast majority of e-book authors do not assign ISBNs to their e-books. Their view is that most of their sales and circulation will be directly through Amazon and Amazon doesn't require an ISBN, so why spend money on something that's unnecessary? That logic is difficult to refute.

In the end, it's a personal choice.

12 — Covers

A book isn't complete without a cover. You can be the best writer in the universe, and it won't matter if people don't pick up your book and start reading it. So how do you entice people to buy your book?

The answer is: with a great cover. Of course, we have probably all also heard the saying, "You can't judge a book by its cover." But, in reality, isn't that exactly what we do as readers? There are a lot of books in the world. Even if you know what genre you're looking for—such as Romance—if you walk into a bookstore and go to the Romance aisle, or you log onto Amazon and search for "Books – Romance," you will still be confronted by an assortment of literally hundreds of books. You only want to buy one—how do you decide which one?

If you are like me, you probably start by simply scanning the covers, looking at the covers and the titles for the ones that strike a chord with you on some visceral level. Once you have identified a few covers that might be worthy of your consideration, then you probably turn over the book to read the blurb on the back cover (in a physical bookstore) or click on the title to read the blurb on-line.

A basic rule for cover design, perhaps especially in fiction, is that you don't want your cover to be too different from other books of the same genre. Obviously, you don't want your cover to look exactly like another book, but you don't want to style or design of your cover to be so radically different from the others in the same genre that your cover looks amateurish or is clearly the odd man out in the bunch.

Book cover design is a specialty so, unless you have some graphic arts capabilities, this is one aspect of self-publishing where it may be better to pay a professional rather than going it alone—if you can afford to hire a professional. Not everyone can afford that, and since this book is about getting your book self-published using nothing but free software, let's discuss ways to create your cover for free.

Many of the low-budget cover artists don't create original art for the covers they design; they download a photo or two or three from the Internet, use a program such as Adobe *PhotoShop* to combine and manipulate the images, and then they paste the title over the cover image. Despite what the "experts" say, a budget publisher who has some sense of aesthetics and composition can create a perfectly acceptable book cover using the free Microsoft Paint or Paint 3-D program that comes with Windows. Most versions ("distros") of the Linux operating system include the GIMP graphics program, which has a steep learning curve but is ultimately much more capable than Windows Paint. And there are other Paint-like programs that can be downloaded for free.

Using Paint has a significant handicap: The text. In Windows Paint, you can create a text box, type in or paste in text, and as long as you keep that text box active you can move it around, change the font, the font size, the font color ... but as soon as you click the mouse anywhere *outside* of the text box, that text becomes an integral part of the image and it can't be re-opened for editing.

That's a problem. One solution is to use the cover creator provided by Amazon KDP when you upload the book body. It works, but the cover generally comes out looking like it was designed by Amazon KDP. I have never been happy with Amazon-generated covers but it's free, so it's definitely worth a look. If you can come up with a cover you're happy with, you don't need to look any farther. But what if you're not happy with Amazon's cover creator?

Instead, how about using the same LibreOffice Writer program you used to write and format the book interior to also do the book cover? The purists will tell you it's just not possible to make an acceptable cover using just a word processor, but the reality is that it's easier with *PhotoShop*, but it's entirely possible using just Writer. The print-on-demand services prefer a PDF file, and Writer can export to PDF, so it's certainly possible from a technical perspective. Writer does have one disadvantage when trying to make a cover for a printed book, which I'll discuss when we get there, but it can be overcome by using Microsoft Paint or any similar program.

Where do we start? As the Red King told Alice in Wonderland, "It is best to begin at the beginning."

The first step, as with formatting the book size, is to set Writer for the page size. But a printed book has a front cover, a back cover, and a spine. Before you can lay out a cover, you have to know the thickness of the spine. That's a function of the number of pages and the paper type, so the interior layout has to be completed and finalized before starting the cover layout. Once you know the number of pages, Amazon KDP offers an on-line cover calculator that will automatically generate a template with all the dimensions you need to know in designing your book cover.

As an example, assume the trim size is 6.0" x 9.0". For covers, we usually want to ensure that the image or background color extend all the way to the edges, so KDP requires 1/8-inch of extra space (called "bleed") around the perimeter. This means the height for the cover will be 9.0+.125+.125 = 9.25 inches.

The width has to include the front cover, the back cover, the spine, and the bleed on each edge. If the book thickness comes out as one-half inch, the total width for the cover will be .125+6.0+.5+6.0+.125 = 12.75 inches. Open up Writer to a new blank document, go into the Format > Page Style dialogue box, and set the required dimensions from the Amazon template (including the bleed) as a custom page size. The page will be wider than it is high, so be aware that if you set the larger number as the width, the orientation should still be Portrait. If you set the smaller dimension as the width, the orientation should then be set to Landscape.

Go to the margins settings and set the page margins to zero on all sides. THIS IS IMPORTANT!

With the page set up, the next step is to import the photo or image you want to use as the background for the cover. You can have any number of image boxes, so it is possible to use one image for the front and a different image for the back. For simplicity, I prefer to find a single photo or image in landscape (horizontal) orientation that has the important part of the image on the right-hand side, and make that my cover image.

Go to the "Insert" tab on the menu bar and click on "Image." This opens a File Explorer window, from which you can navigate to the image you want to use for the cover. Select the image and click "Open." The image will be pasted into the page. With the margins set to zero, the image should completely fill either the width or the height of the cover area. Unless you are very lucky and the proportions of the photo happen to match the proportions of your cover exactly, the image probably won't extend to the edges completely in both height and width.

The image will have small circles at all four corners and on the mid-points of the sides. These are called "handles." If you allow the mouse cursor to hover over one of these circles, you should see it turn into an arrow. Clicking and dragging these handles allows you to resize the image. However, the default setting is for resizing the preserve the proportions of the image. This is called locking the "aspect ratio." If you use the mouse to drag one side smaller, you'll see that the height also becomes smaller.

To get the image to completely fill the cover, you need to unlock the aspect ratio. To do this, right click somewhere inside the image. At the bottom of the pop-up menu, click on "Properties." From the Properties dialogue box, you can adjust virtually everything about the image. To unlock the aspect ratio, go to the "Size" section and uncheck the box to the right of the size fields (the padlock icon should appear to be unlocked). Click "OK" to close the dialogue box, and you can now resize the height and width of the image independently. Drag the handles to the edge of the cover on all four sides.

The most difficult part of getting a cover right is defining the spine area and keeping the text within that. Writer makes that easier by providing a way to draw guidelines that you can use to define the spine. There are two ways to access the line drawing tool: Either click on the diagonal line icon at the right-hand end of the upper toolbar, or from the "Insert" tab on the menu bar click "Shape" > "Line" > "Line." When the line tool is active, a set of windows will appear in the lower toolbar at the top of the screen (immediately above the ruler bar) allowing you to select the thickness and the color of the line.

The back cover will be 6.0" + .125" (the bleed, remember?), so the left edge of the spine will be at 6.125" from the left edge. The top ruler starts at zero, so the first line will be drawn from the top of the page under the 6.125 tic on the ruler, straight down the page. On the bottom edge of the screen there is a box that shows the position of the cursor relative to the left edge and top edge of the page. This makes it easy to start the line and keep it vertical as you drag the mouse to the bottom of the page.

The spine is half an inch wide, so we need a second line at 6.125" + .5" = 6.625. Draw a second vertical line at 6.63 inches. This establishes where the spine will be. Don't worry about the lines ruining the cover—they'll be erased at the end. Remember that there's an eighth of an inch of "bleed" at the edges, and if the book is bound and trimmed perfectly that goes away during manufacture. The actual margin allowance begins an eighth of an inch from the edges. If you need the extra visual guidance, you can also draw in those guidelines.

Once the guidelines have been placed, it's time to enter the text. I typically begin with the title. Once again, go to the "Insert" tab and CLICK "Text box." Place the mouse cursor approximately where you want the upper left corner of the title text box to be, click and hold the left mouse button, and drag the cursor down and to the right to create the text box that will contain the book's title. It will have handles, so once it's in place you can adjust the size, and move it around.

Inserting the text frame opens up the standard word processing tools, allowing you to select the justification (usually center), the font, the type size, and the type color. Type in your title, and make any changes needed to make it what you want. You will be able to return to it and make changes later, if necessary. Repeat this to create a new text box for the author's name, and another text box on the back cover for the blurb and/or a paragraph about the author.

With the title, author, and blurb entered, it's time to add the title and the author to the spine. Note that very thin books won't provide enough space on the spine, so it may have to be left blank. The KDP cover template tells you the actual width of the cover and it also gives the dimension for the spine "safe" zone. This is because the cover may shift slightly during the binding of the book, and they don't want the spine text so close to the edge that the slight shift will result in the text bending around onto the front or back cover. Be sure to keep the safe zone in mind.

To enter text for the spine, begin by creating a new, long text box in a blank area of the front or the rear cover. Type in the title of the book, using the same font as the title on the front cover, but smaller.

When the text is correct, click anywhere outside of the text box to close it. Click (one time, not double click) on the spine text to make the text box active again, then right click and select "Rotate" on the pop-up menu. This allows dragging the text box to rotate it.

Rotating a text box manually is not very precise. After rotating it by approximately 90 degrees, it's time to fine-tune it. Right click on the text box, and select "Position and size" from the pop-up menu. This opens a dialogue window from which the parameters of the text box can be edited very precisely, to the nearest hundredth of an inch. The first tab in this dialogue window is "Position and size." On the right-hand side is a setting for "Anchor." This defaults to anchoring the text box to a paragraph. This makes no sense for a book cover, because there are no paragraphs; all text on the cover is in text boxes. I prefer to change this to "To page."

Then select the "Rotation" tab on the left side of the dialogue window. In the "Angle" field, edit the number to 270.00 degrees, then click "OK."

Use the handles on the edges of the image to drag them close to the text in order to eliminate excess borders. Then drag the text box into the spine safe zone, and use the handles to adjust the size of the box to fit within the spine area. If necessary, click on the text to change the font size until it fits within the safe zone of the spine.

Repeat the above steps to create a text box for the author's name on the spine.

The cover is now finished. All that's left to do is to delete all the guidelines, save , then export it to PDF using the built-in export function, the same as for the book body.

The following image is a sample book cover I created using the exact procedure spelled out in this chapter:

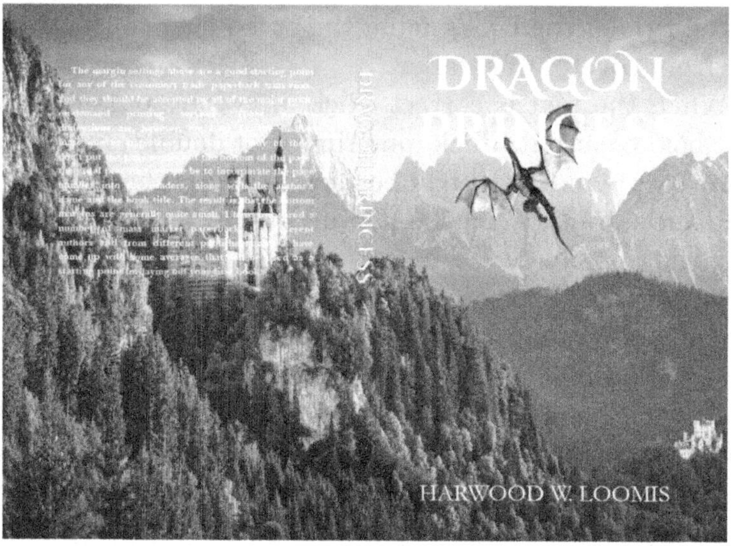
DRAGON
HARWOOD W. LOOMIS

13 — Conclusion

Formatting a book for print isn't rocket science. The difference between a book that looks grossly amateurish and a book that looks like it was designed by someone who knows what they're doing is generally just a matter of paying attention to details that are easily addressed using most major word processing programs.

There are a lot of books for sale on Amazon's web site, so new authors are competing against a huge field. You should expect that prospective buyers will use Amazon's "Look Inside" feature to see what's behind the cover of your book. They can't read the whole story, but they can usually read the first chapter, or at least a good portion of it. The story itself has to be good enough to grab and hold their interest, but how they view the story may also be affected by their subconscious reaction to the appearance of the book itself. If it looks sloppy and unprofessional, that perception is going to color their perception of the story—whether they recognize it or not.

Many years ago, in the auto racing field, Roger Penske became famous for finding new ways to give his teams an advantage. His little ways to gain an edge were always within the rules, they were just things that the other teams hadn't thought of. In any competitive endeavor, you can't afford to give your competitors an advantage. Having a professional-looking book is certainly an advantage. If your competitors are doing it, you can't afford not to do the same. You owe it to yourself, and you owe it to your story.

It is my hope that this book will help new writers to realize that it isn't difficult to produce professional-looking books, so they can compete on even terms with other authors in their chosen genre. Most important, creating professional-looking books doesn't require spending money to buy new software, or using valuable writing time to learn a new software program. Even if you are on an extremely tight budget, by using *free* software such as LibreOffice and the information contained in this book, anyone can self-publish a professional-looking book to Amazon KDP or to any of the competing print-on-demand services with *zero* out-of-pocket expense (other than possibly purchasing an ISBN number).

About The Author

Harwood W. Loomis is a semi-retired architect, ordained minister, clinical hypnotherapist, and author whose technical articles have appeared in a number of trade magazines dedicated to architecture, engineering, and property management. A life-long automotive hobbyist, he has crewed for a stock car racing team, built his own race car for competition on the New England hillclimb circuit, and he is a former state champion in the Connecticut Council of Sports Car Clubs autocross series.

Harwood is a Vietnam veteran. His awards from his service in the United States Army include the Army Commendation Medal, Army Good Conduct Medal, Vietnam Service Medal with Two Bronze service Stars, Meritorious Unit Commendation, Republic of Vietnam Gallantry Cross Unit Citation with Palm Device, and the Republic of Vietnam Civil Actions Honor Medal Unit Citation, First Class. During his Army career he was a member of the 1814 Color Guard and a member of his battalion competition shooting team.

Harwood has served as a member of the board of directors and Vice President of a mental health halfway house; member of the board of directors, author, and contributing editor for the Trumbull [Connecticut] PC Users Group; and member of the board of directors and newsletter editor for The Phenix Society, a not-for-profit organization dedicated to improving the quality of life for senior citizens. He currently acts as a moderator on three Internet discussion forums and writes for and serves as Senior Editor for an online magazine.

Harwood is a widower who lives with his family of Jeep Cherokees and Jeep Comanches in Woodbridge, Connecticut. His house stands on the last remaining portion of a larger tract of land that was granted to a maternal ancestor by King George of England before the American Revolution. He qualifies for membership in the Sons of the American Revolution as a result of service during the revolution by both maternal and paternal ancestors.

To Learn More About Self-Publishing

There is a lot more to successful self-publishing than just the layout of the book's interior. If you found the information in this book to be helpful, you might enjoy my larger book, *The Frugal Yankee's Guide To Self-Publishing*. That book is available in both paperback and e-book versions, from Amazon and multiple other outlets.

https://www.amazon.com/Frugal-Yankees-Guide-Self-Publishing-ebook/dp/B09QLBG9X3/ref=sr_1_9?crid=3TUWK02EZZ2TS&keywords=books+by+Harwood+Loomis&qid=1686999642&s=books&sprefix=books+by+harwood+loomis%2Cstrip-books%2C106&sr=1-9

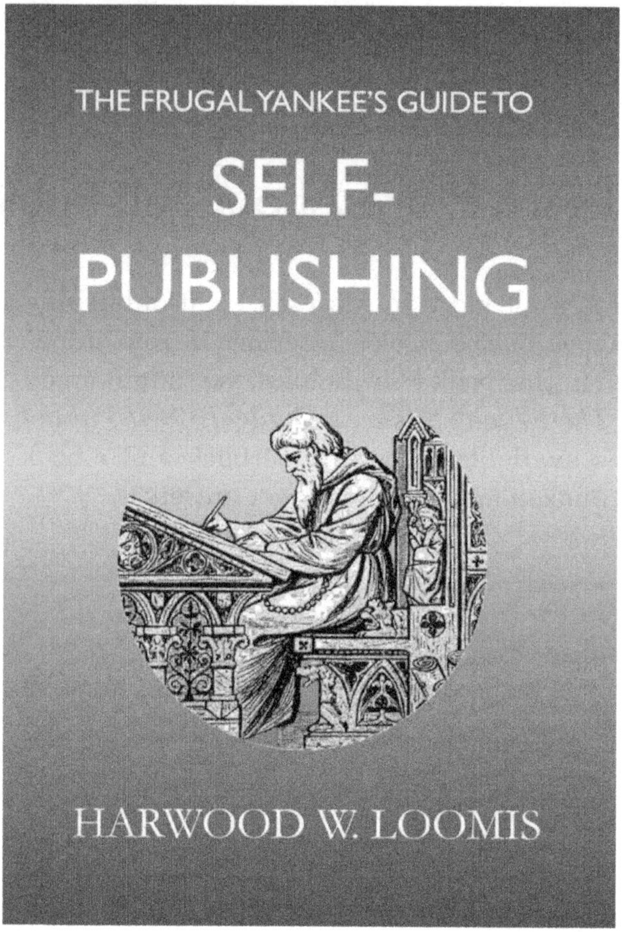
THE FRUGAL YANKEE'S GUIDE TO
SELF-
PUBLISHING
HARWOOD W. LOOMIS

Made in the USA
Monee, IL
04 November 2026

67377386R00085